CW01267418

Civilization

Civilization
How We All Became American

Régis Debray

Translated by David Fernbach

VERSO
London • New York

CNL — CENTRE NATIONAL DU LIVRE

This work was published with the help of the French
Ministry of Culture – Centre national du livre
Ouvrage publié avec le concours du Ministère français
chargé de la culture – Centre national du livre

First published in English by Verso 2019
Translation © David Fernbach 2019
First published as *Civilisation: Comment
nous sommes devenus américains*
© Éditions Gallimard 2017

All rights reserved
The moral rights of the author have been asserted

1 3 5 7 9 10 8 6 4 2

Verso
UK: 6 Meard Street, London W1F 0EG
US: 20 Jay Street, Suite 1010, Brooklyn, NY 11201
versobooks.com

Verso is the imprint of New Left Books

ISBN-13: 978-1-78873-403-5
ISBN-13: 978-1-78873-406-6 (US EBK)
ISBN-13: 978-1-78873-405-9 (UK EBK)

British Library Cataloguing in Publication Data
A catalogue record for this book is
available from the British Library

Library of Congress Cataloging-in-Publication Data
A catalog record for this book is available
from the Library of Congress

Typeset in Sabon by Hewer Text UK Ltd, Edinburgh
Printed and bound by CPI Group (UK) Ltd, Croydon, CR0 4YY

The fate of the human species is at stake. Just as the Hitlerization of Europe would most likely prepare the way for the Hitlerization of the whole world, carried out either by the Germans or by their imitators, similarly an Americanization of Europe would likely lead to the world's Americanization. The second evil is less than the first, but it comes immediately after. In both cases, the whole of humanity would lose its past.
– Simon Weil, 1943

I ask myself whether all this – Europe – will not end up in madness or a general softening of the brain. "At the fourth stroke, it will be precisely . . . the end of a World."
– Paul Valéry, Cahiers, 1939

Contents

Acknowledgements	ix
Note to Reader	xi
1. What Does 'Civilization' Mean?	1
2. When Did Europe Stop Doing Civilization?	17
3. When Did France Become a Culture?	31
4. What Is the New Civilization?	69
5. Why Do We Still Close Our Eyes?	107
6. What Is New about the New Rome?	135
7. Why Is 'Decadence' Pleasant and Indispensable?	167

Acknowledgements

This book has benefitted greatly from the rewarding discussions I have had on various subjects with my friends Marcel Benabou, Bernard Cerquiglini, Jean-François Colosimo, Michel Jarrety, Claude Mazauric, Paul Soriano and Jean-Louis Tissier. To all of them I express my deepest appreciation.

Note to Reader

The use of the word 'America' in the singular and without an adjective may shock the reader. In the expressions 'God bless America' or 'Make America great again', the part is taken for the whole. In Latin America, people speak more accurately of the Americas – Las Americas. 'America' was the baptismal name given in 1507 by the German cartographer Martin Waldseemüller in Saint-Dié-des-Vosges, based on the voyage of the Italian Amerigo Vespucci to only the southern half of the Western hemisphere. The symbolic cornering of its two continents by English-speaking and Protestant America, ignoring the Romance languages and Catholic traditions in the rest of the New World, has since expressed the relationship of forces between them. In what follows, the word designates less a state and a territory than a certain form of civilization.

1

What Does 'Civilization' Mean?

Civilization – a word that sings and is sung in all sorts of scenes. A wandering fairy that evaporates in an iridescent blur. So many reasons to cry wolf. Why should we take account of it again? Because there is no time to be lost – and that vaporous, ethereal, shape-shifting word is covering up a reality that could not be more pressing or more concrete.

Paul Valéry did not want us to waste too much time defining these vague entities, which he knew to be mortal. Let us grant him that it is easier to identify, at a distance at least, a savage than one who is civilized. The former has red skin, a feather through the nose, earrings; the latter is more elusive. A more serious definition would have to suggest, whether we like it or not, a delimited period of time (stopping the meter) and a confined extent of space (a 'here' and no further). Yet the distinguishing characteristic of a living civilization is its capacity for metabolism: it transforms itself as it absorbs and stimulates others. They who would make of it a fixity only mummify a being which in reality feeds on borrowings and exchanges. A civilization also means windows and ventilators, missionaries and merchants. Marco Polo, taking the Silk Road, blew a little Italian air into the Mongol Empire, and a little of the air of Asia into Pisa *intra muros*. The Mexican peon scales the twenty-one-foot fence and learns English; the West Coast must start learning Spanish again. Here, to breathe is to mingle. Isolates are abstractions and isolators do themselves no favours. 'You don't belong here, clear off' amounts to 'let me decay in my bolt-hole'.

Yet we must also admit that even if we are reluctant to draw their outlines too exactly, civilizations do it for us, by excluding one another – covertly or openly. They mix, but they also abrade. The friction between them, aggravated by migration, gives rise to eczema. Here and there, in the face of refugees, demands arise not for borders but their opposite – for barriers of cement, if not indeed barbed wire. The sedentary does not want the nomad; neither does the Wasp want the Chicano, nor the Turk the Armenian or Greek; and so on. It is a long road from globalization to 'happily ever after'. All is nomadic, all is criss-crossed, all is diffused, yes. But not everything can go everywhere. The proof of the pudding is in the eating, and the proof of civilizations is that they do not digest just anything. Fernand Braudel observes that civilizations have invisible customs posts, filtration systems without filters. No bull of excommunication or deportation order is in any way required, so spontaneously does allergy do its work. Italy and the Iberian Peninsula did not let the Reformation in. Shiite Persia blocked Sunni incursions, Arab or Ottoman. Marxism could not be grafted onto the Anglo-Saxon world, with the exception of a few academic enclaves. After two centuries of Anglican occupation, Christians number a mere 2 per cent of the population of today's India. With the exception of the Syro-Malabar Catholics of Kerala, Hinduism held fast: the Gospel made no dent on the Vedas. Hindi has not been defeated by English, and India will remain singular as much as it remains plural, with its twenty-three official languages and some five hundred dialects. The 'American way of life' may have covered the body of Mother India with a mantle of malls and screens, bars and music videos, ring roads and fast food, but it will not find it easy to abolish what amounts to the soul of this breakwater of humanity: wonder at the cosmos, laughter at the joke that is life, which makes of death, for each individual, a comma, not a full stop. In spite of the global market and of consumerism, India has some chance of remaining a civilization, instead of becoming a mere folk culture among others.

'Concrete' comes from the Latin *'concretus'*, meaning solid, consistent, thick, and from the verb *'concrescere'*, to solidify slowly, binding together disparate elements, mortar or stones. The concrete is complicated; and the complicated, discouraging. Hybrids produced by a mélange of epochs do not have a good reputation; the mixed bloodlines of early days offend the bearers of glorious titles, who like to assume clear borders and pure origins, when they themselves are already confluences. Soldiers of Christ the King are liable to grimace when told that Christianity is a dark-skinned Eastern religion, or that it was Islam, its adversary, that introduced them to the Aristotelian legacy on which they pride themselves, received by Muslims from Syriac translators, themselves Christians, from Baghdad. *Ex oriente lux.* Of the Jewish people themselves, to whom we owe so much, but who in turn owe a great deal to Mesopotamia, which gave us writing and the Creator, it can be said that they were born in Egypt, acquired their identity in Babylon and wrote their history in Alexandria. A lineage of memory requires a straighter line. And from what a mishmash comes our Father Christmas with his hood and his white beard, whose effigy was burnt as pagan by a bishop in the forecourt of Dijon Cathedral on 23 December 1951, to general acclaim. Santa Claus arrived from America in great style, but he had disembarked there long ago from Scandinavia – and further back from Roman Saturnalia, and yet further from prehistoric cults like that surrounding the Druidic mistletoe. How many tributaries for a little Christmas tree!

And what zigzags for a proud and pure 'Christian civilization'! From the start, three sedimentations. At the beginning, a Jewish ritual, the scriptural proclamation expressed by Joshua, later called Jesus, namely the reading of a passage of Scripture given a contemporary interpretation, in a Sabbath homily in the synagogue. Then, in the second century, a philosophical movement that integrated this Judaic dissidence into the sphere of Hellenism, in the language and categories of Greece. Then, the third stage in the third century, the incorporation of this theology into the language and law of Rome, allowing it to become the candidate to succeed 'Roman civilization'. This process of growth through transposition, which generated such a successful amalgam, was no obstacle to a denial of debts, bleaching of colours, annexation of creditors, a false birth certificate, all part and parcel of the work of the self on selfhood. If it did not transfigure its history into legend, with beautiful lies and the fabrication of far-fetched, improbable founding heroes – the Japanese goddess Amaterasu, Aeneas or Vercingetorix – a civilization would not be a place of belonging, a home, but an academy of sciences.

Where does the blurred appearance that makes us cautious about them come from? These nebulae are not to be seen with the naked eye. They are meshes of tenuous thread, like a collective unconscious all the better shared for not being conscious; unlike a military alliance or a political confederation, a system without any parts; an unseen, all-encompassing entity, an ethos without ethics, a brotherhood without brothers. Civilizations possess a persistence that can harden beyond expectation when a foreign body attacks them from the outside (witness Arabic-Islamic or Slavic Orthodox reactions today) and soften beyond imagination when the rift is from within (Shiites and Sunnis; Russians and Ukrainians). This comes from far in the past, no one knowing exactly where, and reappears without anyone really knowing why. What insists, persists and *refuses to sign* is a creature that snaps its fingers at our attachment to ideas of copyright. The continuing action of what has ceased to exist – Christendom, the Ming dynasty, the Ottoman Empire – is an offence to common sense. There is something in the very notion of a civilization that is an affront to the forward-looking, emancipated mind – as if it were an unformed thought mistakenly cast in sticking plaster, a hindrance to the freedom of the consumer, or some other millstone. A *we* that can at any moment remind an isolated *me* rebuts the monad that would see itself as self-generated, the child of its own works and sole author of its life, dreaming of the ability to choose a body, a sex, a language, a memory, as it sees fit.

The worst is that this is a conspiracy without a conspirator. It is impossible to shout 'Death to Charlemagne!', who embroiled us with Byzantium, the second Rome, and so eventually with Moscow, the third, over a fairly bizarre controversy (the Holy Spirit – did it just come from the Father or from the Father *and* the Son?); 'Down with Mohammed!', the Bedouin 'coming into our midst to slit the throats of our sons' and our priests; or 'Damn Confucius!', who made China incomprehensible, if not impenetrable, to us. Such outbursts would have little effect. We understand that this ball and chain has often been judged reactionary or fatalistic. Yet those who would make a clean sweep of civilization regularly break their teeth on this thing that is not a thing – elusive, tough and stubborn.

Robespierre and Lenin could have redoubled their efforts, without their activism changing either language or climate, national diet or family model – indeed, all that the passage from horse to high-speed train, from the abacus to the computer, from capitalism to socialism and back again, has left fundamentally unaltered. The Soviet Russian never bade farewell to St Sergius or borscht, any more than a priest-eating Frenchman did to the division of the lunar month into four weeks, a biblical inheritance, or the hour into sixty minutes, a legacy from Babylon. And we are not going to see a Sixth

Republic in France abolishing the Gregorian calendar (the First got nowhere with its republican calendar).

A civilization, wrote the historian Charles Seignobos, is a grid of 'roads, ports and quays'. It is also the way time is divided, and space demarcated; a main course, a favourite colour, a recognizable headgear. Kemal banned the headscarf and the veil, but while the fez disappeared, the hijab resurfaced. The mark of a civilization is a culinary base that no act of will, good or bad, can prevent from rising to the surface of the sauce. Colour prints of Stalin were not presented as icons, nor statues of Mao as a new version of ancestor worship – nor indeed our own Mariannes as so many Virgin Marys without the halo. It would kill the effect to reveal its source, but without the 'paleo' there is no 'neo'. A futurology without genealogy is no more than a ripple in a children's pool.

If pure calculation of interest were to govern our alliances and affinities, it would be logical, to use a contemporary example, for the Russian Federation – rejected by Europe and surrounded by NATO – to make common cause with China, but as even certain Russians say themselves: a marriage of convenience, yes, we can imagine that, but little chemistry – 'we are not of the same family'. As for those who have fabricated a Europe united on paper, pink or blue, ignoring the fault-line that runs from Riga to Split, a fracture inherited from the *Filioque* quarrel that has separated West from East since the eighth century, they have not achieved and will not achieve anything for their pains. No peace conference will dissipate an underlying mistrust and animosity between Arabs and Persians, Hindus and Muslims, even Lutherans and Papists, not to mention South and North Americans. Since every new religion is a heretical version of an older one – Buddhism of Hinduism, Christianity of Judaism, Protestantism of Catholicism, and so on – there is no civilization which has staked its claim somewhere in Babel without opposing another one; the dead lie heavy on the neck of the amnesiac. This *affectio societatis* offers no comfort to beaming notions of world improvement, global governance or other United Colors of Benetton – or for that matter, talk of collective security or cosmopolitan homilies. Everything that unites us also divides us, and it is about as likely that a universal human civilization will come into being – anywhere other than on the podiums of the United Nations or UNESCO – as that an extra-terrestrial with two heads and four legs should deign to land on our planet. Tomorrow is not that Sunday. Plurality is the law of the earth, Hannah Arendt maintained. Fine! But we would do well to remember that this plurality promises as many slammed doors as open windows, as many knives pulled as hands shaken.

Let us first distinguish, then, between 'culture' and 'civilization', these 'sets of attitudes and skills learnt by men as members of society', as Lévi-Strauss termed them. They are too often confused (Hegel took the one for the other). In the Age of Enlightenment, Mirabeau and Voltaire invented 'Civilization' as proper noun, the exit from 'Barbarism'. Germany, a short while later, would oppose '*Kultur*', a living particularity rooted in a people and a soil, to '*Zivilisation*', inert and deracinated, its procedures applicable anywhere. 'Today it is the duty of man to ensure that civilization does not destroy culture nor technology the human being', warned the Berlin historian Theodor Mommsen. And the Anglo-Saxon anthropologists who with good reason translated moral idea into social fact, reserved 'culture' for primitive societies and 'civilization' for modern ones. So there is a good deal of interference on the line and fog on the road. Let us try a clarification.

What distinguishes 'the first and most complex of the permanent forms of social life' from others that might at first glance appear more readily visible, like the tribe, the nation or the state? First, spatially – by the range of their diffusion:

Islam in one variety or other extends from Dakar to Jakarta. Here foundations are wider than the structures that are built on them. Then, temporally – by their longevity: Rome lasted a thousand years, China is nearing its third millennium. Their depths are not easily broken. China has seen many a dynasty, many a massacre and many a great helmsman, and may see others. But its pagodas will still be there. Storks pass; steeples remain.

No culture without agriculture, no civilization without the city. Etymology distributes vocations. Here a locus, there a topos – in each case, a mould capable of accommodating, and of shaping, several catchments. Even if the most intensive cultivation is beneath the walls of a city, or close at hand, it can always return to compost – it is rural. A civilization, on the other hand, is carved in stone – it is urban. It needs centres of accumulation and redistribution, and urbanization cannot occur just anywhere. The shores of the sea and the banks of great rivers, which allow the cheap transportation of goods and commodities, attract it quite naturally. More propitious for cultures, sensu stricto, are mountainous zones difficult to access. Steppes, massifs and high plateaux encourage a particularist resilience. Geography is a home port for one, a springboard for the other. A culture remains single, while a civilization has children. The first is to the second what a kingdom is to an empire – or a retrenchment to a propagation. There is, for example, a Basque culture, bringing together seven provinces straddling the Pyrenees border, but it stops north of the Adour and south of the Ebro: it does not seek to encroach on Gascony or Aragon. Many Basques have emigrated, their descendants populating Latin America; St Ignatius of Loyola and St Francis Xavier were far from sedentary; but the *pelotari, chistera* and *trinquet* (player, glove and court of the game of pelota), the *makila* (shepherd's staff), the *pastorale* (psalmodic theatre), smuggling, berets, *piperade* (dish made with peppers) and, first and foremost, the enigmatic Basque language, the true criterion of belonging, have one kingdom and only one: the Basque Country. Basque culture, like Yezidi, or, more accurately, Kabyle or Aymara, does not want anyone treading on its sandals, but equally it does not step on anyone else's. Basqueness adheres to Basques, and no one else. It seeks no sphere of 'co-prosperity'.

No need, on the other hand, to be born in Italy or a champion of the Pax Romana in order to speak Latin and think like a Roman – as St Augustine, a Berber, or Thomas Aquinas did. No need either to have an American passport, or even speak fluent English, to adopt US manners and customs. As a mother tongue irradiates into regional dialects, so a civilization opens out the culture from which it originates – the Sinosphere includes China, Japan, Mongolia, Tibet, Korea, Vietnam, Singapore. A civilization contracts when its forces begin to decline. This retraction or clenching, which signals a retreat, is called a culture. Hellenic civilization extended to the Indus, Christian from Patagonia in the west to Kerala in the east, the faith of Hejaz spread across Byzantium and Persia to North India. Buddha, born in India, crossed the Himalayas into China, but the Mediterranean was forbidden him, Zoroastrian Persia blocking his missionaries to the west by a tissular incompatibility. A civilization is not made by spontaneous generation. A culture constructs sites; a civilization builds roads. It presupposes and requires a foreign policy. A civilization acts; it is offensive, unlike a culture, which is defensive and reacts. The correct term would really be '*civilizaction*'.

Let us take heed of this '-ion', the suffix of action, the action of the great city on its hinterland, the *urbs* on the *ager*. There is no civilization that is not rooted in a culture, but this does not become a civilization unless it also has a fleet and an ambition, a great dream and a mobile force. In that sense, Pericles represented the moment of culture in the Greek world and

Alexander its moment of civilization. A little empire, that of Philip II of Macedonia, was necessary between them. English Puritanism, a local culture, planted the seeds of a civilization across the Atlantic, and American neo-Protestantism has now crossed the ocean in the opposite direction, to spread the American way of life in Africa. When a root acquires wings, it can create branches *extra muros*. Such wings do not grow all by themselves.

A language or a religion, or still better a mixture of the two, can create a lasting encampment: Hebrew and Judaism are a case in point. A civilization demands more: an empire (Abbasid, Carolingian, Spanish, British, American ...). And whoever says 'empire' also says 'armed force', as whoever says 'army' says 'war and conquest'. Local cultures also sometimes have to take up arms, to survive or to be reborn, but these are wars of necessity, defence or liberation. A civilization practises war by choice, wars of invasion or colonization. No Hellenism without hoplites, no Islam without cavalry. No Christianity without Templars, no Ottomanism without Janissaries. A funny paradox: the antonym of 'barbarism' always has pools of blood in its baptismal fonts, St Bartholomew's Days without which civilization would not be what it is. Like every other, Christianity has an embarrassment of choice in matter of ethnocides: from the massacre of the Hierosolomites (1099) or the Albigensians (1209) during the Crusades, to the annihilation of pre-Columbians in the mid-sixteenth century and the extermination of Amerindians three centuries later. Civilizers with clean white hands do not exist: all have a black book in the drawer. A regional dialect could, at the end of the feudal era, attain the status of national language by equipping itself with cannon and a centralized monarchy (as with François I in France). But the inventors of cartography (a mark of civilization) would sooner or later need triremes, gunboats or aircraft, to not just reach other shores but camp on them. That is expensive. Taxes have to be levied, ports opened, forests planted, engineers recruited, along with blacksmiths for the cavalry.

'Imperial civilizations' are a pleonasm. Just as an empire is multi-ethnic, a civilization in the prime of its life needs every talent available and will make satellites out of a number of cultures, be these enclaves, outposts or relays: Nepal and Indonesia are not India, any more than Vietnam or Mongolia are China, or today's Italy, France or Mexico are America. A spaghetti Western has an Italian flavour, and primaries in France cost less than in the States (our 'participant finance', with dinners at €7,500 a head, is fundraising on the cheap). The modulator can be modulated; to each partner their unit of measure. A nebula requires more than one star.

The American model is a paradigm in this respect, in its capacity to project both forces and forms outwards. Beyond the first circle of the family (Great Britain, Australia, New Zealand, Canada and the United States – the absolutely trustworthy countries sharing a single intelligence system, the Five Eyes), its centre of diffusion radiates in all directions, with bridgeheads on five continents, and a rosary of skylines, megalopolises new or renovated, functioning as antennae – or so many 'free zones', gated communities in the global village. Tokyo, Singapore, Dubai, Tel Aviv, Lagos, Lima . . . In addition to these 'civilized' coastlines, some others above or behind them are cities that subsist on culture, from Kyoto to Kuala Lumpur, Mecca, Jerusalem and Cuzco. For all that is globalized requires its local colour. If a civilization has its multiples, these are neither clones nor mere replicas. When a civilization is at full strength, it acts like an inflected language in which every foreigner can create their own hyphened version (Italian-American, Chinese-American) without jettisoning their particular baggage. Of the current formula that globalizes a very specific local profile, we have an Arabic version, abstemious and deluxe (Abu Dhabi); an Israeli version, high-tech and muscular (Tel Aviv); a Sino-Asiatic version, crowded but orderly (Shanghai); a Latino version that is borderline and disorderly (Panama); a crazy, congested African version (Johannesburg). This archipelago is united by business and commerce, but since an economy by itself has never made up a civilization, it must satisfy a certain number of other requirements: a film festival, a museum of contemporary art, an annual art fair, an economic forum, architectural feats (the highest tower, the longest bridge), shopping malls and six-starred hotels. The United Arab Emirates, in just thirty years, have fulfilled all their obligations save one: no love parade.

To return for a moment to the hard kernel of a civilization: military force, which is a necessary but not sufficient condition, always needs the enhancement of an imaginary to fire hearts, storehouses to fill stomachs, and a magisterium to occupy minds. Imposition by force – military, financial or both – is ineffectual without the radiance of a symbolic code which alone has the power to make the dispersed pieces into a whole. The equation for 'empire' is Aristotle plus Alexander, Thomas Aquinas plus Louis IX, Descartes plus Louis XIV, Adam Smith plus Admiral Nelson, Kissinger plus General Westmoreland. A form of thought, plus a force de frappe. If Attila had brought a philosopher along in his baggage-train, the grass would have grown after he passed over it. Why were not fulgurating charges of cavalry enough to leave a furrow? Because the Hun, the Mongol and the Tatar were better at mastering space than traversing time, which requires a lute as well as spear and horse. The artist or architect, writer or musician or gardener may all be needed.

The Red Army won the Second World War against Nazism; the United States won the peace that followed. The Soviet Union had a constellation of garrisons and missiles across Eastern Europe and Central Asia after 1945, but no communist civilization capable of transcending and federating stand-offish locals emerged out of it. Moscow lacked nylons, chewing gum and hot dogs, to say nothing of Grace Kelly and Jackson Pollock. The United States lost no time in outdoing the USSR in the matter of arsenals, but if to their 2,000 military installations spanning five continents had not been added 35,000 McDonald's in 119 countries (including 1,500 in France), a language ideal for machine translation, the Gillette razor, vinyl records of saxophonist Lester Young (the 'Prez') and Marilyn's cleavage, there would be no American civilization today. The panoply of weapons is only half of the programme: one cannot sit on either bayonets or missiles. A desirable way of life must not repress, but imprint and invent. Stakhanov was not Bill Gates. Able to do ill, but first to do good. In short, a supremacy is established when the imprint survives the impress, and the impress the imperium.

To measure the vitality of a civilization by the yardstick of its industry or its currency is the myopia of an economist. The United States is deindustrializing, its trade deficit widening, its social inequalities increasing, but its imprint capacity is no more affected than is its firepower, and we can expect that the twentieth century will not be the last to be associated with the name of a nation. Its physical and psychological means of extrojection, military strength and patriotic faith, have in no way disappeared; they remain resilient and are even resurgent. Wealth does not mechanically produce domination: in 1945, the US accounted for two-fifths of global GDP, but its civilization had not remodelled the cultures of the world as it has today. The twentieth century was American: but after the golden age comes the age of silver.

There is too the role of religions in these dynamics of overseas expansion. Yesterday's French empire propelled its colonial projects forward with Catholic missionaries, as did the Spanish empire in the Americas. The English had Anglicanism; Tsarist Russia, Orthodoxy. The American empire has a plethora of neo-Protestant sects for relay – Mormons, Adventists,

Jehovah's Witnesses touring the worlds of Africa and Asia. Established religions are strategic in a double sense, playing defence and offence simultaneously, acting both as frontier guards (Poland, Greece, Armenia) and as advance parties (Liberia, Senegal, Indian outposts). They allow a ritual adhesion, not demanding formal allegiance. The Pentecostal in Nigeria, as in Aubervilliers, swears no oath to the stars and stripes, but involuntarily adopts a way of life and thought born in California in 1906 – a model in turn descending from English Methodist stock of the eighteenth century. Such monotheist cults are clearly tigers in the tank built for export, since preaching and conversion are consubstantial for them. One does not become Hindu; one is born so or one is not. Shamanism does not carry; it remains in Siberia, or in the Sioux reserves. But anyone, anywhere, can become Christian or Muslim. Judaism dropped out of competition after a few centuries of proselytism among Khazars and Ethiopians. Its two monotheistic scions with all their variants could substitute humiliating allegiance with exalted participation. Universal religions are serviceable for both irredentist defence and messianic advance, the survival of a culture and the destruction of others.

A civilization has won when the empire from which it arose no longer requires imperialist measures to imprint itself. When it no longer needs helicopter gunships to control what goes on below. Nor a fist on the table to attract universal attention. Victory can be declared when, instead of *one*, there is only *the* civilization, its language a lingua franca and its currency a common measure. When it can withdraw to its homeland and still be a beacon. When allogenous tribes adopt its tics, its habits and its norms, without even being aware they are cut-and-pasting them. When the commander no longer needs to command. A civilization has won when all that it shapes has become natural, and when it is unbecoming to try to reconstruct the actions that allowed such civility to impose itself, or ask what system of forces lies beneath established norms. When the particular becomes the universal, the philosopher will say. Or for the sociologist, when domination becomes hegemony. Put simply: when there is no longer anything to discuss, and an essay like this begins to seem a little suspect.

2

When Did Europe Stop Doing Civilization?

The short period that can be seen, symbolically, as beginning in 1919 and concluding in 1996, is between two major publications, two benchmarks: 'The Crisis of the Mind', by the Frenchman Paul Valéry, and The Clash of Civilizations, *by the American Samuel Huntington. The difference – the gaping chasm – of views between these two watchmen on the same ramparts illustrates more than a change of paradigm: it is an astronomical revolution. Between these two dates, the earth and the sun switched places.*

Paris, 1919, *La Nouvelle Revue française.* Under the heading 'La crise de l'esprit', Paul Valéry placed human civilizations in perspective, in two successive letters. Comparing France, England and Russia with Elam, Nineveh and Babylon, he took the pulse of the 'European Hamlet' and questioned its future. 'Will Europe become what it is in reality – that is, a little promontory on the continent of Asia? Or will it remain what it seems – that is, the elect portion of the terrestrial globe, the pearl of the sphere, the brain of a vast body?' Remarking, among other subjects for amazement, the contrast between the tiny size of the British Isles and the immensity of India under the British yoke, and more broadly, between the centre and the periphery, he forecast a rupture of equilibrium between them due to the gradual change in their internal relations. Sweeping aside the pious lies still in circulation, about the 'dialogue of cultures' and the 'international community', the former copywriter for the ministry of war went straight to the point: the state of the living world may be defined by a system of inequalities between the inhabited regions of its surface. This inegalitarian system had so far worked in favour of the Europeans. It would shortly swing the other way. We would soon retreat from the front of the stage. And a certain idea of man along with us.

'We others, civilizations ... we now know that we are mortal.' The incipit of this memento mori makes an ideal starting point for any essay on any subject. Two or three generations of students at the élite academic institution Sciences Po have fed themselves well on it. One might believe that this old saw does not deserve any better. The best authors always have these spare parts attached to their name, baggage to which they will owe a posthumous echo that is far from kindly (and better for them if they had no idea of this in their lifetime). Everything fades, everything goes, everything breaks – good business, Mister Poet! I was wrong, and I was not the only one. Wrong not to have read the continuation or taken the development seriously. That would have spared us bitterness and disillusion, even today. The meter reading of 1919 has nothing in common with a bland 'Madame is dying, Madame is dead',[1] the pompous *De profundis* that we might have feared from the Bossuet of the Third Republic (as he mockingly called himself). It is stimulating, precise and clairvoyant. Valéry detested nationalism – his article was published first of all in English, in the London *Athenaeum*. This was the pure water of Europeanism *avant la lettre*, unimpeachable, without a word against conquered Germany, without the least flattery towards the Allied nations, whom Valéry realized were already secretly suffering. All in the same boat, with the route escaping the majority (but not Albert Demangeon, a modest

---

[1] From a well-known funeral oration by Jacques-Bénigne Bossuet, for Princess Henrietta of England in 1670.

geographer and author in 1920 of *Le Déclin de l'Europe*, nor Drieu la Rochelle, the unhappy author of 'Mesure de la France', 1922).

Could this very mantra not be recited without closer examination? First of all, *civilizations* is written in the plural and without a capital. We leave behind the railway of the nineteenth century, with its top level – Civilization, one below this – Barbarism, and one at the bottom – Savagery. It would be inadvisable to see these as disjoined sequences, where once you are ahead you can no longer fall behind: there is a barbarian asleep in every civilized person. And so, let us refrain from smiling; humanity has more than one product in its stores. That is reassuring. There is a choice in stock, and a new order on the way; the winter of one civilization is never more than the springtime of another. Let us remain calm. And then, it is not so much the word 'mortal' that is out of kilter (after all, we all die one day), but rather the awareness of this. Successive civilizations in the prime of life naturally see themselves as insurpassable and superior to any other. The sentiment that the baton will some day have to be passed on only dawns at the hour of retreat, in that fine moment of lucidity, recapitulation and withdrawal that is wrongly dismissed under the name of decadence. This reframing in a longer temporality makes immediate life more precious and more intense. We should dry our tears. Finally, Valéry's most meritorious word was 'now'. In 1919, all of France was exultant. It had won the war, its army was the best in the world, it had colonies over five continents, a language at its zenith, an industry and an agriculture. The first intervention of the United States on European soil was seen in 1919 as no more than military, with no more than temporary consequences. A peace congress in Versailles redrew the map of the world, and three of the four powers involved were European (England, France, Italy). To sense, at the apex of this pride and insouciance, that in reality the age spots were already apparent showed a certain boldness. Nothing is more risky than to be the contemporary of one's time, nor more remunerative than to be its dupe.

This forecaster in the guise of a poet was an astonishing breaker of dreams. He had only disdain for history as a scholarly discipline, a 'wretched conjectural science', and meticulously avoided the pitfalls of his age. To understand the force field of the wide world required turning one's back on the squabbles of the day. Indifferent enough to the gossip of his village, but crossing the cities of Europe and familiar with its chancelleries, this offbeat character, whose head was never turned by the cretinizing wind of success, described everything that would happen without prescribing to anyone – no one could be less of a preacher. Always a step ahead in the games under way. In 1897, he had explained the how and why of the new German predominance in Europe, signalling to his English friends that it would make life difficult for them, and it was indeed the confrontation of these two imperialisms, rather than one of nationalisms, that gave rise to the First World War (the marriage counsellors of the former 'Franco-German couple' would do well to cast an eye at this X-ray). His *Regards sur le monde actuel*, published in 1931, and that each passing year made more topical, exposed the cogs of a globalization under way, with the interdependence of nations that resulted from this – the 'conquest of ubiquity'. He foresaw in 1928 the arrival of television in the home, with 'distribution companies providing palpable reality', and already noted the inconvenient side of generalized zapping – 'from now on the eye relishes a crime, a catastrophe, and hurries on'; he heralded the levelling of the strong and the weak in the world arena – with 'the growing technical equalization of peoples' (as would be confirmed by the equalizing atom, then digitalization, and finally cyberspace). This was his 'theorem of levelling'. At the same time as 'the rapid and fantastic growth of means of communication', he foresaw 'an unforeseen invention that may change tomorrow all the conditions of economic and military power' – the bomb launched against Hiroshima. He predicted the tilt to the Pacific and the 'pivot' towards the ocean of the future. He sensed 'an extreme instability of the world equilibrium', with 'multiplied chances of conflict' – the Second World War. Valéry had no degree in sociology, but to announce in advance these unforeseen events, adding that 'Europe visibly aspires to be governed by an American commission, its politics is tending in that direction', we have to agree that he had flair (*Notes sur la grandeur et la décadence de l'Europe*).

Valéry's Europe was certainly not ours. In his eyes, it included all the people who had experienced three influences: that of Rome, with its institutions and laws; that of Christianity, with the ideas of conscience and the dignity of the person; finally and above all, that of Greece, which 'has distinguished us most profoundly from the rest of humanity', having given us, with its axioms and theorems, the only true universal, that of pure science. As a consequence, 'Wherever the names of Caesar, Gaius, Trajan and Virgil, of Moses and St Paul, of Aristotle, Plato and Euclid, have had a simultaneous significance and authority, there is Europe.' What needs to be added to this résumé? Influences from Persia (Love and Evil), from the Celtic world (the sorcery of Mother Nature), Arabic ones (numbers), not to speak of the Enlightenment (the critical eye). The fact remains that strong doses of this chemistry have been received well beyond the Eurozone. And when the old pilgrim, after having done so much to give spiritual content to a geographic expression, sums up his route in these words: 'Europe will not have had the politics of its thought', we cannot but agree with him, half a century later, with a lump in the throat. And go and bend over his grave, in the sailors' cemetery at Sète, his birthplace, where his verses are engraved on the tomb: 'What better reward after a thought / than a long glance on the calm of the gods.'

Valéry does not give the word 'spirit' the meaning that

'artists, poets and women' give it. It is neither a supernatural entity nor the faculty of reason. It is less than anima and more than animus. Spirit is a *power of transformation*, or a certain quantity of energy, combining psychology and thermodynamics. A civilization in progress transforms its surroundings in its own image, and when it comes to be transformed by manners, passions and rituals that are no longer its own invention, it withdraws into a culture. It is when a society becomes less imprinting than imprinted, less initiating than receptive, and the balance of its exchanges with the environment falls into deficit, that the countdown sets in, and its life expectancy can be predicted.

What is most significant is that our clinician never speaks of the *West* (a word Valéry used only in his preface to a Chinese poet). The concrete entity whose submersion he glimpsed has only one name: European. He sees no other in the West that might lay claim to an equivalent exemplary status, the highest degree of complexity yet attained by the human biped growing in age and wisdom. That said, our child has a child of its own, 'a nation deduced and as it were developed from Europe' – a promising *projection*, if still rather hesitant, whose distant presence reassures our troubled Europe, in the guise of a lifeboat or spare wheel. That is America. Valéry's *Cahiers* of 1939, on the eve of the Nazi invasion, are evidence of this. He sees America as what we would today call a panic room. And we are in debt to the Americans for emerging from their great island to seek out some of our valuables and place them in security, first among them Varian Fry in Marseille, who embarked André Breton, Max Ernst, Claude Lévi-Strauss, Victor Serge, Anna Seghers and others towards our Noah's ark. Ungrateful little France that, rescued in this way, has not even given the name of this hero to an avenue, a museum or a library.

This is how the mappa mundi was modelled and painted by the most level-headed spirits before the war, without partisan bias. The German Edmund Husserl (1859–1938), another key witness, did not draw it differently in his celebrated Vienna lecture of 1935, 'Philosophy and the Crisis of European Man'. The thesis would have been disturbingly ethnocentric if the founder of phenomenology had not given the notion of Europe a transcendental sense, as a figure of historical becoming, rooted in factual reality, but outgrowing this in width and depth. Like Valéry, Husserl did not doubt the identity of essence between Europe and its American branch office. 'In the spiritual sense', he wrote, 'it is clear that to Europe belong the English dominions, the United States, etc.' An 'etc.' that included South Africa, Australia and New Zealand – same level, same calibre. Our great men, who – alas for them – had probably never heard of John Ford or Louis Armstrong, nor danced the foxtrot, ridden in a Buick or a Chevrolet, or bought a Singer sewing machine, would have been quite amazed to learn that twenty years later the dominion would be Europe itself: internal autonomy, but delegated sovereignty. Their benign neglect towards America, however, in no way meant hostility. It had nothing in common with those French essayists of the period – Charles Maurras, Joseph Kessel, Georges Duhamel, Bertrand de Jouvenel – who snobbishly despised 'that titan of the material world, which has remained Lilliputian in the spiritual order'.

On the far right, with Ordre Nouveau, Jeune Europe and the 'conservative revolutionaries', jibing turned to phobia. Books such as *L'Abomination américaine* by Issac Kadmi-Cohen (1930), *Le Cancer américain* by Robert Aron and Arnaud Dandieu (1931), and *Lignes de chance* by Henri Daniel-Rops (1934) denounced 'the result of the mechanism causing the death of everything in man that denotes originality'. Our own two geopoliticians refrained from any value judgement. Holy war against 'rationalist error' and the 'invasion of mechanism' was not their hobby-horse. America, in their eyes, had as much spirit as Europe, for the simple reason that it was the same. Consequently, they did not see the detour via this residential suburb as necessary. Nothing essential of one's time was lost by remaining on one's own promontory. Neither Valéry, Husserl nor Picasso ever went to America. They count among the last representatives of a Europe in which it was possible to make a name for oneself at home, and a fame abroad, without ever setting foot in the United States (which would be suicidal today for anyone who sought to gain a place in the sun – no longer the Riviera, but the Sun Belt).

We might almost wish to whisper retrospectively in the ears of our two Cassandras the warning of a US secretary of state, Dean Rusk: 'If you don't pay attention to the periphery, it changes and becomes the centre.' One should never underestimate one's acolytes and children, and our patriarchs failed to appreciate the divine ambitions of the New World, the son of the Old Testament. For the new Puritan Israel that fled the kingdom of England, as its Hebrew predecessor had fled Egypt, Europe represented Evil, and Evil has to be opposed.

Washington, 1993, in *Foreign Affairs*. Under the title 'The Clash of Civilizations', Professor Samuel Huntington devoted an article to the partition of the world into 'large geopolitical spaces divided by fractures'. Full of a variety of reflections on 'the civilizations of yesterday and today', their global policy, and the West vis-à-vis the rest of the world, his article, developed in 1996 into a book, became a global bestseller, its resonance multiplied by 'Nine Eleven'. An added subtitle then was 'and the Remaking of World Order', and the retrospective description of civilizations led up to the prescription that the West would have to gird itself to maintain the respect of the jealous hordes at its gates.

We shall not dwell on the objections already made to these

gut-level geopolitics. The fragility of a rather rustic parquetry and overly self-interested recommendations (the Catholic-Protestant bloc of the West rejecting the Orthodox of the East). We can also leave aside the accusations of war-mongering, imperialism and colonialism that have been levelled. To try and convince the elders of the Western club that there are other civilizations than their own is in no way reprehensible, if it can stop them reading and writing 'the West and the Rest', a formula used in Pentagon memos. To signal to our consuls that 'the rest' is not a coarse hotchpotch, prey to the worst devilries, that it is also entitled to its gods and its rites, is a welcome proposal. Such great flattening needs some touching up, but what fresco does not? One might point out the existence of Suriname, a Muslim state, with its Malays and Javanese, in the middle of Catholic Latin America, and alongside it Guyana, a member of the Organization of Islamic Cooperation. Or again a white tribe, the Boers, in the far south of black Africa. We might recall that the same religious identifier has never prevented conflict, and that fratricidal wars are the worst, Sunni against Shia, Catholic against Protestant. And that the Greek and Russian clergy, both Orthodox, dispute the leadership of eastern Christians. In short, one could argue provocatively that everything Huntington writes is false, apart from his central intuition: beneath many contemporary confrontations, and far below and beyond economic interests or political struggles, there is something archaic at work. Which should incite the children of television who govern us to better study history and geography before intervening in affairs that are foreign to them.

Faithful to the best traditions, Huntington reprises the traditional cataloguing, an almost botanical inventory of civilizations past and present. The English historian Arnold Toynbee counted in the course of history more than twenty civilizations, including five principal ones in the nineteenth century (Islam, China, Japan, India, the West). The German philosopher Oswald Spengler made it eight (Babylonian, Egyptian, Chinese, Indian, Meso-American, Greco-Roman, Arab and Western), divided into three classes: magical, Apollonian and Faustian. Fernand Braudel distinguished thirteen major existing civilizations, including four European (Latin, Greek, Nordic and Russian). For Huntington, whose presentation of the question is most up to date (at least chronologically), there are seven or eight: Western, Latin American, Islamic, Chinese, Hindu, Slavic-Orthodox, Japanese, and possibly African). European as such has disappeared, divided in two and absorbed by 'Western'. And his copious critical apparatus ignores Valéry, who would likely have received his posthumous disappearance with a smile, as we now know that we are mortal.

There are clearly other reasons for this erasure: topicality is in command, and expresses itself in English. We can add: the influence and noise of American analyses. Empires, these complicated states, have the art of simple ideas. The weak haggle, the strong strike. *Imperatoria brevitas. Veni, vidi, vici.* Why so succinct? Because 'everything that is simple is wrong, and everything that is not is useless'. And so, anything that simplifies our view of the world propagates itself a thousand times better than anything that complicates it. This is the cunning of America's 'simplification committees', which distribute worldwide the uselessly sophisticated works of learned Europeans. If their scaffolding was not crude, would it be seen from afar? It is perhaps up to us, useless rhetoricians, to re-educate ourselves from these great mediators, instead of always splitting hairs and complicating the issue. The Roman recycler of Greek subtleties was similarly apt at ridding them of their pearl grey mannerism, embellishments and nuances. Geometry is Greek, but surveying is Roman. To spread the good news, you always have to get down to the nitty-gritty. Did we not do the same ourselves with the New Law, simplified to the extreme so as to transmit the profundities of the Old? God knows that the Old Testament is richer in characters, adventures and false bottoms than the vade-mecum of our catechism. If Francis Fukuyama can remind a Texan oilman of the existence of a certain Alexandre Kojève, or Huntington remind a New York trader of Fernand Braudel, should we not rejoice? The expansion of the potential audience is worth a few losses along the way.

Let us not be old-fashioned, sticking to the delicatessen against the supermarket. What is disturbing is how Valéry was forgotten by his own people, in France itself, when this subject came onto the agenda. Our colloquia, articles, debate and polemics on this fashionable theme discuss for and against Huntington. References and deferences have taken over the land of the setting sun. If it is a question of recalling the action at a distance of one body on another, known as influence, it is Joseph Nye and his 'soft power' that are cited rather than Gramsci and his hegemony, something far more substantial. If the 'end of history' is mentioned on the Left Bank, another classic from the repertoire, then it is immediately Fukuyama who appears. And Kojève disappears, the Parisian philosopher from Russia whose pre-war seminar on Hegel's *Phenomenology of Mind* was seminal (a seminar attended by Aron, Bataille, Lacan, Queneau among others). Mr Fukuyama may not be 'a Hegel for children softened up by Disney Studios', as an overly bitter or demanding colleague said of him, but he is certainly easier to read. Our criteria: second-hand success, well marketed, rather than original scholarship with a small circulation. What then happened so that the hotel annex has become the palace for all of us? For celebrities such as José Ortega y Gasset, Salvador de Madariaga, Aldous Huxley, Oswald Spengler, Ernst Robert Curtius, Charles-Ferdinand Ramuz, Romain Rolland or Curzio Malaparte no longer to be referenced in their own countries, evacuated from magazines and ignored by the pens of our ministers and presidents? For the ideas that count being those from the Hudson, and no longer from the Thames, the Seine or the Tiber? Let us admit it: in 1900, a well brought-up American was a European in exile; in 2000, an up-to-date European is a frustrated American – or one waiting for his visa.

The permutation of mutual dependence has been concealed beneath an evocative purple cloak – the West. By this is understood a Euro-Atlantic space with elastic edges that groups together the 'community of democracies'. The spray of scent consoles the European side for its recent relegation and protects the American side from any petty resentment. A neat psychological trick (learned from Hegel: the zeitgeist is a cunning worker). The link of subordination vanishes automatically, as it's a matter of nice buddies and a great cause. The West has its aura, between mystical and poetic, a shivering and imperious aspect that casts opprobrium on any prosaic examination of the lines of command that tie, for example, the so-called North Atlantic Treaty Organization (since extended to the Pacific, Central Asia and the Middle East) to the White House, the only place from where any order of mobilization can proceed, a responsibility of which the holder is beginning to tire. A visiting card with no plan attached, no organogram or supervisory board, the West has up till now conveniently fulfilled the immemorial function of myth, which is to change history into nature and contingency into self-evidence.

When we look at the overpopulated earth of 2017, with 4 billion inhabitants simply in the zone stretching from Kabul to Japan – Asia has 60 per cent of the planet's population, and 34 per cent of world GDP – we might well shrug our shoulders. At a time when a fully reawakened China is buying up our power stations and airports, when an Indian businessman gives his name to our blast furnaces, when the spectre of Muhammad walks our streets and America seems to shake in its shoes, the question of knowing who in the 'Western' couple wears the trousers may seem of local interest, and purely retrospective.

A quarrel over seating in the salons of the Cercle Interallié [an élite social club]? Or a dispute among shareholders of a multinational in difficulties? With this passing of the torch, this transfer of the baton of command and study, far more is involved than a matter of self-esteem. By becoming the holder of the patent on 'modernity', without anyone taking note, the Americans put themselves in a position to set the rules of the collective game, by showing the laggards what kind of life and what human type is worth imitating, and how to behave so as not to miss the bus. International bodies no longer ask emerging peoples to Europeanize, but rather to Americanize. By ceding to courts across the Atlantic the arbitration of what is right and proper, what distracted or docile Europeans have conceded is the world secretariat for the organization of life (in our own sphere). One *patron* of humanity, in both senses of the word ['employer' or 'patron saint'], has expelled another.

As a consequence, while in 1919 there was a European civilization, with American culture as a variant, in 2017 there is an American civilization, in which European cultures seem, for all their diversity, at best minor variations, and at worst indigenous reservations.

On the chessboard, this is called castling. On the battlefield, it is called defeat.

3

When Did France Become a Culture?

If a dominant civilization can be compared to an inflected language, a dominated culture can be compared to an uninflected one. French no longer reigns in France, because Homo economicus, whose native tongue is English, now reigns here, with a direct and rapid link from the capital to the Capitol. Which changes both the form of cities and the spirit of mortal men.

Nothing that man has is ever definitely acquired, neither love nor civilization. For example, the small Asian kingdoms such as Indonesia and Kashmir that were first Hinduized and then Islamized, or instead Buddhized, like Nepal, had to reinsert their culture, hiding or smuggling it, into a wider ecosystem that subsequently arrived, in a way that saved the furniture and saved face. Culture then functions as a retrenched camp forced to negotiate with the new guardians. It often happens, in fact, that an old civilization, caught in the mainstream of a new and better offer, has to withdraw into its 'national identity' like a security fence. It develops a narcissism of little differences, stylizes its totems, theatralizes its accent. Contemporary France seems to have adopted this logic of survival. Astérix shows his muscles in a country worried about its spelling because it is losing itself, and because the son of an executive in 2015 makes five times more mistakes than the son of a worker in 1930. 'If you had not already left me, my dear soul, I would not pursue you on my tribunes or in my laws. If your spokespeople did not have a vocabulary of two hundred words, if my president did not say "*faire en sorte que*" every two sentences, do you believe that article 2 of the Constitution would lay down that "The language of the Republic is French"? You would have neither my sighs nor my flashing headlights.'

For example, since Montreal has mutated into a North American city like any other, Quebec, by way of reaction, has exhumed the fleur-de-lis, voted for law 101 that makes French obligatory for immigrants, cultivated its *joual*,[1] its singers and its poets. Mexico, towed along in its lifestyle and mode of consumption by its great northern neighbour, emphasizes its Aztec features so as not to become a sub-America, with a panoply of museums, tacos, *charangos* and Frida Kahlo. And in the kingdom of France, the Puy du Fou[2] is fully booked. Our imaginary community, a fiction continued by way of a constraining reality, brings out its family jewels, Versailles, Amélie Poulain's[3] rue Lepic and place du Tertre, restoring its châteaux, its Marais and its heritage, with the TV soap *L'Amour est dans le pré*, Roquefort and the *Petit Nicolas*.[4] The art of living, fashion, good taste, the countryside. Bordeaux and Burgundy. Tomorrow will see the return of Georges Brassens, with appropriate songs on the local radio stations. And the imperfect subjunctive will flourish in the learned societies of the Périgord. The 'French touch' has a future.

Homo economicus

The triumph of *Homo economicus* both characterizes and sums up the new age. He is taken for granted, strident and

---

1 The popular language of French-Canadians.
2 A historical theme park in the Vendée.
3 The heroine of the eponymous film, set in Montmartre.
4 A series of children's books, depicting an idealized French childhood in the post-war years.

offensive in the American republic, being almost its very foundation; derivative and second-hand in the French republic, which is doing its best to match the American model. The kingdom of rhetoric has quietly joined the empire of statistics. In the beginning was the Word. In the beginning will be the Number.

Counting there has always been – heads of cattle, vine stocks and regimental soldiers. Accounting arrived with stock-raising and war; it goes back to the Neolithic age. The digital revolution, which codifies any fact whatsoever into binary notation, clearly plays a large part in this qualitative leap of the quantitative. But if data and big data are today the keys to the 'final secrets', this needs to be put into perspective. It is not a coup d'état, but a blow against the state. *Homo economicus* has dethroned *Homo politicus*, who for three centuries had headed our legends as well as the junior staff, and had himself, in the Age of Enlightenment, removed *Homo religiosus* from his pedestal. Christianity transmuted religion into politics; the French Revolution turned politics into religion; the accounting age makes economics both its politics and its religion – a synthesis that deserves consideration.

It is a confusing situation that the very time when the 'end of ideologies' is celebrated should see the triumph of the most inclusive ideology of all, economism. In the Middle Ages, a large swathe of life escaped the grip of the clergy and its divine commandments; but what part of our own life can avoid calculation? Our electoral campaigns are battles of '*chiffronniers*',[5] but even sensitivity now has its quarterly index. According to a survey by the Institut Think, the French happiness index in 2016 rose from 5.9 to 6.0 on a ten-point scale, with a fall in depression of 0.3 points and a rise of 0.3 for projected 'satisfaction of life in five years' time'. Adversity

---

5 A neologism punning on '*chiffre*' (number) and '*chiffonier*' (rag-and-bone man, now archaic).

also has its rates. As do the anxiety and expectation of the indirect – so-called 'recoil' – victims of attacks compensated for by guarantee funds, pro rata according to the degree of kinship, the emotional tie or the delay involved. For any kind of injury, the insurers of sentiment will calculate a profit. 'I am unhappy, anxious about death, you owe me so much.'

There is a move for schoolchildren's attendance in classes to be compensated, and the farsighted envisage the crisis in reading for pleasure being remedied by a subsidized body of public readers. We are all now expected to 'put a figure on it' – an expression that is incidentally incorrect, given that the figures in our numbering system are equivalent to the letters that make up words. Medical staff are assessed by the number of interventions they perform; traffic police by the number of tickets; prefects by the number of expulsions; police by the number of charges brought; and researchers by the number of publications: publish or perish. Feed the beast or die. More is better. The ambiguity of the bestseller. Bookshop sales figures serve as awards, from the better at the top to the worse at the bottom. A publication no longer has to be judged by its readers, or by discussion among them. It will be evaluated by the number of 'references' or citations made to it. For the human sciences, the qualifying database operates automatically: number of articles published in (English-language) scholarly journals, and number of occurrences in the citation index.

Ideology. An ill-famed and above all ill-formed neologism, borrowed by Marx from the French *'idéologues'* of the eighteenth century. It suggests that an ideology is made up of ideas, like a wall made of bricks or a preserve from fruit. The reality is far less complicated, and still more unstoppable. The word simply denotes what a given society agrees to hold as real, at a particular point in its evolution. Without reflecting too much on the question, since the answer is taken for granted and the scale of reality coefficients remains unquestioned. For St Louis the instruments of the Passion had greater weight than the sickles and hammers of his ploughmen. In the thirteenth century, it was in the beyond that serious things happened. Charles de Gaulle held that a distinguished scholar was more important than a tax inspector, and a great writer more important than a large employer or a movie star. For us, what weighs most is a level of debt or a growth forecast. And in a century or two, this will appear as hard to understand as it is for us that a Norman knight, fully in his right mind, would go and suffer a thousand deaths on the road to Jerusalem to take possession of an empty tomb. One fairy tale follows another, and the only thing they have in common is that they are not to be questioned.

Aside from a handful of the socially inadequate, who persist in granting some reality to invisible and incalculable things, nothing is more convincing in our eyes than a statistical curve, or more eloquent than a computer graphic, in other words a visualized measure (see screens and magazines). The figure that kills, in the marketplace, has replaced the word that kills (you don't destroy what you replace); and we no longer edify our fellows with quotations, but instead with percentages. *Rem tene, verba sequentur*, 'stick to the thing, the words will follow', as Cato advised an apprentice public speaker. Today he would whisper *numerum tene*, and you'll have it in hand. Quantity is no longer just a check, but an injunction; polling less a thermometer than a compass. The algorithm does the work, programmed by the cost killer.

Marcel Mauss had a presentiment of this back in 1924: '*Homo economicus* is before us.' He has arrived, and is now on top. Seeing the insults exchanged between schools and experts, Diafoiruses,[6] negationists or henchmen of capital, we may wonder whether economic science deserves this name.

---

6 After Thomas Diafoirus, the archetypical pedant portrayed in Molière's *Le Malade imaginaire*.

This parascientific battlefield, despite its arithmetical apparatus, does not resemble the experimental or exact sciences. However fragile their knowledge, its champions always act the part of primus inter pares: over-employed, overvalued, rushing in all directions, but dominating and sure of themselves. Marx, in his desperate condition, can be proud of himself: he has defeated his free-enterprise conquerors, who have only abandoned religion, the one-time opium of the people, for a still more effective drug. A shame that this piety does not pay greater attention to mathematicians. The death of the greatest passes unnoticed.

This fundamentalism has an excuse, avenging the unjust contempt in which stewardship was held by our old captains. Gripped by remorse, their successors bend the stick in the other direction in an attempt to put it straight. And so enterprise is today the beating heart of society. A schoolteacher, the head of a university, a hospital manager and a heritage administrator are all supposed to behave like corporate directors. Likewise, the politicians in charge of 'France PLC' and its annual accounts, in the public sector just as in the private. Business and governance are now one and the same. This pure and simple fusion seems amply confirmed. 'When interviewees were asked who is the most useful to society, 88 per cent replied the head of a small or medium-size company, 62 per cent the managing director of a large corporation, whereas politicians reached no more than 16 per cent', *Les Échos* reported in autumn 2016. Statistics have spoken. The acrobats who juggle with figures above our heads operate with a safety net.

France is generally seen in Europe as the political country par excellence, with England holding the palm for commerce, and Germany for industry. In unkempt Gaul, the state constructed the nation, contrary to the case in Italy or the Netherlands. This is a handicap to overcome. A deputy fears losing her job, a government minister who resigns boasts of 'reducing the market share' of her president, and a (Socialist) minister responsible for innovation declares that 'when you do politics it's like doing business, you have to be judged on results'. This is the view of *governance*, a term borrowed from the business world. In 2008, French ministries were inspected by an American firm, Mars & Co, under contract with the state, and each given a merit rating – administration assessed by the standard of the private sector. The Anglo-American ratings agencies, manufacturers of figures deemed more legitimate than the inspectors of finances established by the Revolution, give ratings on a daily basis to our governments of the number, by the number and for the number. In politics, programme has become supply. And each of us manages our love affairs, our career, our wallet, our children and our neurosis. Hegel, for whom every totality was good, and who deplored the divorce that Christianity had made between Heaven and Earth, would have rejoiced at the sight. We have reconciled the two: value and size are one and the same. The totality of human existence is covered. Tell me how many followers, likes and posts you have, and I will tell you what you are worth. There is not even an intellectual, an entrepreneur of ideas, who does not convert himself into the head of a counselling agency. 'Politics has become powerless and disappointing. Intellectuals have understood that the real power lies with corporations' François Ewald, once close to Sartre and Foucault, declared to *L'Expansion*. The *libido dominandi* has joined the logic of business.

Difference in scale does not spoil the appetite for conformity, contrary to what Valéry believed in 1919. In terms of volume, France was and remains in relation to the United States what the Banque Lazard is to Goldman Sachs, Monoprix to Walmart, France Télévisions to Netflix, Léon Zitrone to Walter Cronkite, *Les Rois maudits* to *House of Cards*, Nanterre to Harvard and Johnny Hallyday to Elvis. By and large, a ratio of one to five. In content and form, France broadcasts on the same wavelength. We used to have learned societies, now we have think tanks. In the *Global Go To Think Tank Index Report* (2015), France lags behind, but it is on the way up (1,835 think tanks in the United States, but already 145 in our own country). If we cannot compete on equal terms with the RAND Corporation, the Heritage Foundation, the Brookings Institution, the Hoover Institution, and so on, we hold steady for all that. In the 1960s, the Club Jean-Moulin attracted top civil servants; in the 1980s, the Fondation Saint-Simon[7] brought together officials and businessmen; in the 2000s, the Institut Montaigne, with its summary memos, proceeds from the top down, from financial groups to ministers and company directors. And the reclassification of Sciences Po as a business school has been greeted as a success.

De Gaulle, referring to Joan of Arc, spoke of the 'honour of being poor'; Nicolas Sarkozy: 'Afterwards, I'll make a packet.' The fact that we French, fearful and low-paid savers, are not more annoyed with the money men must be seen in this perspective as an advance. The old Catholic cant, which the early socialists inherited, was unable to resist the salubrious gospel of prosperity. The taboo is raised, Père Grandet[8] buried. We talk money at dinner, how much do you earn, my council tax, 15 per cent reduction. If some people still lambast 'King Money', which 'rots even the consciences of men'[9] – and enlist Léon Bloy or Léon Blum on this subject – it is just for the gallery; at bottom, no one sees sin in a Rolex, Fouquet's, or a soft-top Maserati. Vulgar indeed, but actually more

---

[7] An influential neoliberal think tank, founded by François Furet in 1982.

[8] The miserly father of Eugénie Grandet in Balzac's eponymous novel.

[9] De Gaulle once said that 'king money' was his 'only enemy', François Mitterrand in 1971 that it 'rots even the consciences of men'.

crippling. With the help of *Forbes* magazine and its local imitators, we have learned to watch the prize for the hundred biggest fortunes in France with the same eye as the annual list of Légions d'Honneur on 1 January. Emancipated, to be sure. Money makes us free, and there is no freedom without inequalities, these being only the overhead costs. Already our egalitarian demands sound like Robespierre, and the legendary rich see fit to raise the morale of the poorer. We only ask that our future enlighteners be careful of the susceptibilities of the stubborn French people, refraining from too many golden parachutes or mouth-dropping stock options. The backward do not catch up from one day to the next. You have to give them time. The chrysalis does not become a butterfly with a wave of the hand. The old-fashioned will be 'civilized' or revitalized in a few decades, whether with fuss or with applause.

The troubles of Hibernatus

History is not set like a watch. In certain periods, the second-hand hurries; in others it dawdles. The same goes for the metamorphoses of a country. In France, Stendhal was sure he was witnessing a change in our ways of being, one that he saw as unprecedented and exceptional. 'In historical memory, never have a people experienced, in their customs and their pleasures, a more total change than that between 1780 and 1823.' What would he have said of our dangerous triple jump in half a century? It is our particular privilege, thanks to our year of birth, to have been able to witness this in person. We should give thanks for such an opportunity, something that the foolish Polycarpus, a Syrian Christian martyr, did not understand when he cried aloud: 'In what century, my God, have you made me live?' Just imagine the godsend it would have been to have been born in Lutetia under the pagan king

Meroveus, to kiss St Genevieve and to die in Paris under the baptised Clovis; or, for a contemporary of Sophocles born at the foot of a painted, festive and polytheist Parthenon, to see with his own eyes, before falling senile, Greece dressed in black, monotheist and Byzantine.

France has not only, in the blink of an eye, replaced its farmers (26 per cent of those employed in 1955, 2.9 per cent in 2002) with '*rurbains*',[10] the local shop (87,000 in 1966, 14,000 in 2003) with the supermarket (1 in 1957, 10,500 in 2000), and full employment with a high unemployment rate (1.7 per cent of the active population in 1965, against 10.2 per cent in 2016), but has also multiplied fifteen-fold the number of its students (150,000 in 1950, 2,400,000 in 2013). Household refrigerators have increased from 7.5 per cent in 1954 to 100 per cent in 2000, not to speak of washing machines (8.4 per cent in 1954, 96 per cent in 2000), while 97 per cent of households have televisions (1 per cent in 1954). We have not only invented a new age of life, adolescence, replaced the housewife with the working woman, and increased the number of centenarians from 200 in 1950 to 18,000 in 2017, but life expectancy for men has risen from 60 for men and 65 for women in 1946 to 79 and 85 respectively in 2016. Among other achievements are the changes in the shapes of towns and the hearts of people, things not found on the Internet but in a special personal memory. At this point we need a change of register.

This story is about a certain oddball (1940–2017) whom we can call Hibernatus. He was twenty years old in 1960, when he left his adopted Latin Quarter for new horizons, and after being *cryogenized* (a miracle of biotechnology) was fortunate to wake up defrozen in the City of Lights in 2010. He had reached an age when it is easier to remember one's childhood than what one did the previous day. So our

---

10 Semi-rural, semi-urban.

Hibernatus was an involuntary 'Mr Yesterday', a 'despite ourselves' of the retrograde army, who tried to recognize the quarter where he had grown up, with a view to finding his bearings and getting back on track.

Starting his morning walk in the Luxembourg gardens, he was perplexed by the spectacle of a dense column of out-of-breath individuals, men and women, old and young, scantily clad, running along the fences, some calm and collected, but with their tongues hanging out. Collective punishment? A local marathon? He had no time to find out, as when he reached the bottom of the rue Soufflot, which leads to the Panthéon, towards the great men and *'la patrie reconnaissante'*, he could not recognize the two propylaea at the crossroads. In place of Café Mahieu (where the waiters were distinctly unfriendly, reserving their welcome for members of the Légion d'Honneur) stood a McDonald's, and on the other side, on the Place du Capoulade (which he used to favour) was a Quick ('Quality Burger Restaurant'), advertising a special offer on its Mega Giant. The visual shock could be absorbed, but there were others to come when he descended the Boul'Mich. Two-thirds of the shopfronts were clothing, with signs in English or a dialect approaching this. In a row, Derhy, *'very good* offers' in red letters, HP Caterpillar, New Shop, Luxury Outlet. One optician called OnOptic, another Optical Discount, one SAGA Cosmetics, another The Body Shop. A tobacconist by the name of Alter Smoke. The patisserie Pradier displayed in its window a 'minute take away'. Hibernatus walked back and forth without flinching, past Marks & Spencer Food, Starbucks Coffee, Gap (a clothes shop) at the corner of the rue des Écoles, GapKids below it and GapBody above – normal, almost classic. But the real blow to the stomach was halfway down, where the great bookshop of Presses Universitaires de France, where professors and students would come several times a week to refresh their minds by perusing the new arrivals, had been replaced by a luxurious Nike boutique – the finest of all. The photo displayed in the window of a tall black athlete had the slogan over it, in big white letters, 'Are you running today?', reminding the passer-by of his duties in terms of speed (which explained to Hibernatus the press of people in the Luxembourg), along with a close-up of an Apple Watch, engraved 'NRC' (for Nike Run Club). 'Back to basics.' Feet first. And timing.

Hibernatus continued on his way, passing the Cluny museum, enclosed by a hoarding with the inscription 'Welcome to Medieval World' and an arrow 'Entrance this way'. Curious to see again La Joie de Lire, the François Maspero bookshop (4 rue Saint-Séverin) where he first learned his way around the planet at the age of twenty, perusing at random all kinds of subversive pages in Spanish, Italian, English, Romanian, and so on, he crossed the Boulevard Saint-Germain and hit upon a Celio clothes shop – 'Enter on your right'. Greatly shaken, Hibernatus felt a slight hunger pang. Noticing set back from the street a little HD Diner, with the promising slogan 'Back to the Fifties (Best Burgers and Shakes)', not far from a Vintage Standards, a fur shop displaying an illuminated sign proclaiming 'Europa first opening', he collapsed into this café and was foolish enough to mechanically ask for a *jambon-beurre*: 'Sorry, sir, we don't have that, but the hamburgers are made in-house.' OK. With a jet of ketchup on top, the multilevel sandwich proved excellent.

Our disoriented hero's head was spinning, and he tried to make sense of what he had just seen. The renewal of contact had been a rude awakening, but, all things considered, not a total puzzle: the Balzar brasserie and the Le Champo cinema were still where they had been. Likewise, the statues of Montaigne sitting and Auguste Comte standing. The Gibert Joseph bookshop (despite more stationery) continued its watch, as did the Métro entrances. The bit of the city he had just crossed was like a former lover seen thirty years later.

'Neither quite the same / Nor quite someone else'. An in-between. A mixture. A compromise. And not just any such. Hibernatus (who had a good visual memory) remembered having passed, at the top of the boulevard, a Nicolas wine shop, set between a New Shop and a Texto shoe store, and lower down a boutique for Basque products (artisan conserves, foie gras, crystallized fruits). There was a Maison de la Lozère in an adjacent side street. And, right on the boulevard, a shop for fine lingerie (there was a second also, but with a 'Miss Coquines' embellished by a little heart over the door). These three were the only ones to have kept their original signs. The disorienting language plunged our revenant into perplexity. The quarter was now Latin only in name, but if the Boul'Mich had been civilized in his absence (no more and no less than other parts), business there continued to honour French culture, with its two pillars so internationally respected and non-aligned: gastronomy and gallantry, and the language of Molière as ornament and foil. With their differential language as their very stock in trade, these boutiques probably had little interest in *globish*. The question remained – a terrible one that Hibernatus could not answer – whether French, in this place of emblematic outreach, was displayed by two regional representatives (Lozère and the Pays Basque) only as a sign of solidarity with another regional language – all wedged together – or as the effect of a vague historical survival.

The dive in which he found himself was *in* and *flashy*. As strokes of fortune never come singly, he noticed a daily paper on a nearby table. This was *Libération* – fewer readers, but the right ones. Hibernatus opened it licking his lips, greedy to make up for his arrears on cultural matters (the downside of hibernation being that the biological clock gets out of sync). But the more he turned the pages, the more he felt out of the action. He hardly understood a word of the idiom used, except that it had broken with Stratford-on-Avon in favour of Frisco and L.A., which Hibernatus had never had the occasion to visit. Unsure that he would ever catch up with the times, which were tearing along too rapidly, he returned home and went to bed, shattered. The Paris he had known had undergone a serious facelift. It was too much for him. The only answer: a big sleep.

The next day, a little revived, he returned to this question of language, and certain memories came back to mind. A comic book, *Parlez-vous franglais?*, by an irascible purist named René Étiemble, who had made a name at the age of twenty denouncing 'a plague that delivers us to Yankee imperialism' (the very expression now sounds outdated). Long before the 'show', the 'self-service' and the 'surprise party', this grumbler sounded the alarm. To say 'maintenance', 'manager', 'sponsor', 'parade' and 'strip-tease' instead of *'entretien'*, *'directeur'*, *'mécène'*, *'defile'*, *'effeuillage'*, to declare a lift *'hors service'* rather than *'en panne'*, to speak of the *'médias'* or the *'caddy'*, appeared to the eyes of this pterodactyl, who had listened to a lecture or two, capitulation in the midst of the battle. Hibernatus smiled. The 'devastating gibberish' of the 1960s had become old French for the e-generation of YouTubers and gamers, habitués of the Paris Games Week (annual trade fair for video games), of 'battles' and 'fashion weeks', who would 'finalize' a film editing and spoke 'cash'.

As our old prodigal son recalled having himself wielded the pen (though never a keyboard, sad to say) and read Braudel's dictum that 'language is 80 per cent of French identity', he tried in the following days to find out more about what was called *la francophonie*, a subject that had interested him in very distant times. Since the Agence Universitaire de la Francophonie (AUF), which has been most productive in this cat's cradle of committees, commissions, 'high advisory bodies' – who has ever come across a low advisory body? – and state secretariats, had its office close by on the Place de la Sorbonne, he made an appointment with certain old acquaintances who worked there and agreed to receive him. The welcome was rather chilly. They reminded him of certain offensive sallies he had launched in a previous life ('Which one?', he foolishly asked, not remembering any), for example having once compared the offices of official *francophonie* with a Resistance delegation in Vichy's Hôtel du Parc – fourth floor, last door on the right.

'My jokes will be the death of me', Hibernatus said once again. He profusely apologized and swore that he would from now on put himself in the service of these admirable sentinels, always on the alert as they make their rounds. They explained to him that 60 per cent of the teaching at Sciences Po was now dispensed in English (the course on cultural policy in France went under the heading 'Cultural Policy and Management'); that every year fewer heads of state or government attended the ultra-boring 'Peace, Democracy and Human Rights' babbling at the annual *francophonie* summit; that the famous editor of the most recent report on the economic consequences of the use of French had titled his NGO PlaNet Finance (subsequently, Positive Planet); that the French president and his ministers do not give a damn about it, despite saying the contrary; and journalists likewise, though these do say what they think; that industrialists, commentators and communicators, just like the Métro and the bus companies, had happily jettisoned the *loi Toubon* of 1994 on 'the use of the French language'; that in any case, the grammar and language of the Internet were English, as were those of the hard sciences, aviation, sport, the Institut Pasteur and international congresses of history; and finally, that bodies assessing scientific research were North American in nine cases out of ten. After which, the said sentinels made a hastily departure to attend the terminology commission, telling him not to miss the next general assembly of the 'L'Avenir est au Français' organization.

This militant abnegation filled Hibernatus with confusion, making him still more eager to remedy his mistakes. Admiring these men and women, who were perfectly aware of the disdain their hierarchical superiors had for them, he felt that he found himself on familiar ground: a country in which the art of governing consists in speaking loudly and volubly while doing little and the opposite.

Hibernatus promised himself that he would sign the standard petitions and enjoy the expected harangues. Though he wondered whether his friends and himself, by doing what was necessary 'in defence of the language', were not digging in behind the Maginot Line. Not because they were bad generals, but because they were French and thus Cartesians, not really with it, 'it' being the bodily soul of the terrestrial and carnivorous mammal. Apollo's disdain for Dionysus, in other words the intellectual's disdain for *soul* or the grammatical rejection of *swing*, had left a sour note. Our literati had paid little attention to the record bins with their golden, platinum or diamond LPs, or nowadays to the hits on Fun Radio, to electro, funky hip-hop, rap and house, this continuous background leading boys and girls to an El Dorado with no semicolons or past participles agreeing in number and gender. Man was a rhythmic animal, a dancing being, before speech was invented; the thinking reed beat time, and *beat* was not the strong point of the lands around the Loire. It was Afro-American. Rhythm and blues. The video clip and the edited cut led the dance. Faced with the triple threat of song, dance and play, grammatical purism was a thin entertainment. New York's 42nd Street, with its musical comedies and tap-dancing shows – an excellence readily exportable and filmable – had crossed our haughty *linguisteries* as easily as General Guderian's tanks crossed our casemates in 1940. *Singin' in the Rain*, *My Fair Lady*, or the marvel of *Cats* went straight to the marrow, the plexus, the balls. Where things are imprinted, marked and sculpted, where decrees, orders, commissions and recommendations have never been able to bite: the joy of the body. Like Imperial Guard – which dies but does not surrender – awaiting Marshal de Grouchy, so our academicians were awaiting the lexicologist who would give the words of the tribe back their freshness, but instead we had Marshal Blücher: the disc jockey with sampling and gimmick, moonwalk and gangsta rap. The guardians of the dictionary found themselves sidelined. They deserve our homage for giving us *'ordinateur'* [computer], *'courriel'* [email], *'télécharger'* [download], but these were only consolation prizes. Finally, Hibernatus said to himself, if by chance the peripheries reached the centre, and France was definitively on the margins, perhaps this Francophony would take back the banner.

These reveries, unworthy of a serious man, did not prevent the former student and teacher from continuing on his spree (blowing his own trumpet was his Achilles heel). Remembering the cradle where he was de-formed, the Sorbonne, he made his way towards this alma mater. The deterioration of atmosphere and souring of character were undeniable. In his former sphere, the humanities (but not only here), there was grumbling or pawing the ground. Collapse of level, lack of consideration, failure of authority, mediocrity of salaries. The mandarins had disappeared from circulation. The smartest of them improved their purgatory by an annual stint as visiting professor at an Ivy League establishment, or a lecture tour. A well-deserved bunk, which Hibernatus in the early 1960s would never have imagined possible in his case, but had now become custom. The jackpot was an academic chair in proper style. Without making the connection, he discerned in the young generations of researchers a rather disconcerting turn of mind. They all sought to be specialists in something or other, whether in the early Jules Barbey d'Aurevilly or the late Ernest Renan, with a view to recruitment by European studies departments in Chicago, Tokyo or Melbourne. They seemed averse to overall views, which to their minds were the hallmark of the amateur, if not the charlatan – the essayist, we might say. A true professional had his last and stuck to it. He was employed in a particular department and maintained a distanced relationship with his thesis subject, competent but without passion. A phrase from André Gide came to mind: 'X is intelligent but he has the air of having come across ideas rather than having extracted them from himself.'

If he chanced to mention to these rising stars of tomorrow's élite the names of Roger Caillois, Albert Thibaudet or Emmanuel Berl,[11] a kind of pitying amazement appeared on their faces. These social dancers with their light heads failed to see them. This proclaimed withdrawal to their own bit of sidewalk did not fail to astonish Hibernatus, even while the talk everywhere was of *interdisciplinarity*. It is true, he corrected himself inwardly, that one can let oneself be moulded while vaunting 'the broad spread of cultural expressions', a national inconsistency. He discovered whence arose his misapprehension: the imprint of Taylorism based on the division of tasks and the benefits of fragmented work, which a Michel Foucault, returned from the US, drew on to propose the model of the *specific intellectual*. 'Remember that general culture is a bourgeois idea', he wrote in his notebook. A medical friend reassured him. Specialization affected every profession. The generalist was no longer held in much esteem. 'In 1950', he was told, 'there were fifteen surgical specialities. Today there are a hundred and fifty. Science advances.' Hibernatus understood that he too, if he wanted to establish himself, would have to settle down, put up a copper plaque and stop roaming around left and right. Since he still had a vague memory of the link between generous ideas and general ideas, this perspective made him a little sad.

Discouraged by the declassification of teachers in the new age, though every new state of things always has its losers, and being still interested in the life of the mind, Hibernatus was curious to know whether things were not better outside the

---

[11] All wide-ranging essayists influential in the post-war years.

lecture halls, among the famous and the visible. He was forced to accept, after a few days of observation of these pinnacles, that here too the ranks were depleted. A reclassification had been carried out on Parnassus – eternal pyramid of reciprocal envy and disdain – with a system of protocol and precedence that he did not immediately adjust to. Belles-lettres, manifestly relegated, no longer occupied the heights, literature had slipped to the side, and philosophy, its younger sister, no longer reigned supreme over the human sciences, as it had in the time of Proust, Bergson or Sartre. Historians, for their part, had reached the heights, closely followed by anthropologists. Hibernatus recalled the scant consideration that literary lions, in de Gaulle's time, had had for the petty figures of sociology, political science or economics (at a time when in *Normale lettres* on the rue d'Ulm, aspiring prefects who aimed to 'do ENA', and who would today go to HEC, fell into a black hole of total contempt on the part of the fellows).[12] The dukes and peers, cosseted and decorated today, were the economists, followed closely by lawyers.

Topsy-turvy, but was it not society itself that had put itself arse above head, Hibernatus still suspected, still too much of a tourist to grasp the logic of this reversal: the pre-eminence of market specialists in a completely market society, and the prestige of lawyers in a contentious society, where nothing any more escaped legal action – from dental treatment to soldiers killed in combat, from family relations to falls off the playground swings. What interested Hibernatus at this stage was etiquette: not to confuse *noblesse de robe* with *noblesse d'épée*, to limit his gaffes, smile at those you should smile at, and not waste time with pains in the neck who could not be used as footstools. Observing on social occasions who spoke with whom, he soon detected where the seating arrangements and

---

12   References to the École Nationale d'Administration – where top civil servants are trained – and the HEC Paris business school.

ribbons, rosettes and awards came from: from the newspapers, rather than from academic juries. The press pumped up the respective visibilities of all involved (length of TV interview appearance or column inches). He understood that without a professional card in his pocket, or several mates in the game, he would not get very far.

What also bothered him, while strolling through the streets in this age without terrorism, was the disappearance of uniforms: no more soldiers in battle-dress, no more priests in soutane, no more nuns in wimples. General crisis of headgear. The Algerian war was a distant memory. Numbers had apparently dwindled, for both berets and dog collars. Vocations likewise, and pride. The institutions had folded up their sails and veils. Perhaps there were parallels to establish, since he found the same slippage, from theology to morality among Catholics, from vocation to job among soldiers, from justice to ethics among progressives, from nation to profit among conservatives. Collectives had atomized, and there was a competition for the largest pay packet. The fact that there was no longer a marshal in the Panthéon, nor battle plans of Hannibal or Napoleon in the history text-books, particularly distressed Hibernatus. Not that he had forgotten the often unpleasant role of cocked-hatted blimps in our public life, but he had the memory that the Republic rested on two indissociable pillars: the army of the nation and the school of the people. If the one faltered, the other was bound to feel the shock. If the two collapsed together, then a page would surely be turned, which rather frightened our phantom walker.

It hardly helped matters that he was from the left (with its tough respect for traditions). The rudest shock was before him. He noticed this by expanding his patrols to political circles, which were now rather scarce. Under the Pont Mirabeau flowed the Seine, and alongside it our love affairs as well. The vocabulary had changed, at least with the official representatives, and he started to watch his own, fearing to be taken for a Neanderthal escaped from the museum. There was no more talk of bourgeoisie, nation, state, class and class struggle, united front, labour, capitalism. Instead, democracy, civil society, citizens' initiatives, visible minorities, identity. Used as he was to outdated and still dangerous 'isms', struggling to overcome anachronistic reflexes, Hibernatus mentioned one day, in speaking to an oily committee director, the fate of the 'proletarians'. The furrowed brow of his interlocutor immediately led him to correct himself: 'I meant the workers.' 'You mean the disadvantaged milieus?' In sum, Hibernatus had a lot to do to get back in the game.

He was not an incorrigible person, martyr or zealot, but a well-behaved chap able to make allowances. He learned therefore to say 'supporter' instead of *'militant'*, 'fan' instead of *'sympathisant'*, 'leadership' instead of *'direction'*, and 'coach' for *'conseiller'*. Soon the language of sport had no more secrets for him. One day someone spoke to him of rising to the 'first division', probably meaning a deputy's seat, but he still felt too lacking in skill to convert the try. To be truthful, he had realized that public affairs were now a matter for professionals, and that politicians no longer had to be men of knowledge and study. The pros wanted pros, communicators, pollsters, statisticians, spin doctors. The bridges between thought and action had been cut, but perhaps it was better so, he thought; the master-thinkers had done so much harm, it was no accident that the churches now needed no theologians, the parties no serious magazines, the trade unions no researchers into social rights. The precautionary principle was now imposed on all.

Understanding at all events what direction the wind was blowing, he took the side of the centre, in other words, modernity. He liked the *'première dame'*, a function previously unknown, but 'first lady' was the obligatory term. He admired

Sarko One, the president's new plane; was proud of the French Pentagon at Balard, and spoke of the citizens' reserve as our Garde Nationale.[13] He found it excellent that the conservative party had rechristened itself 'republican', and bad that its alter ego had yet to call itself 'democrat'. Had not socialism adopted a great programme for the future, a society of 'care'? One day he was quick to complain to a telephone employee when asked for a 'valid ten-figure "number"'. And when one of his friends, campaigning for the rejuvenation of France, asked him by SMS if he had a mind-blowing proposition for his candidate, he put forward the original idea of 'community organizing'. This would mean basing oneself on local religious and ethnic communities, to have the young 'leaders' of the future emerge 'bottom up' from the real people of the base. This 'management' of a civic initiative had given excellent results in Chicago, he explained to his recruiter, whom he found rather more reticent than he had expected.

As far as the future of humanity is concerned, the stakes had risen. They had become at the same time biological (a different species), arithmetical (you need only count) and legal (with sanctions). He realized this while attending an umpteenth conference on the defence of the language, when boos were heard in the hall as the speakers on the platform were revealed to be three men and one woman. This was the wrong result. The unhappy speakers had to promise those present that quotas would be respected the next time, that the fault would not be repeated. Hibernatus remembered the visits he had made as a young man to the ground-floor apartment on the rue Victor-Schoelcher, and how Simone de Beauvoir had won him to her cause on a basis of republican universalism. Female watchdogs were not yet on the agenda, but de Beauvoir's magnum opus *The Second Sex*, exported to

---

13 In 2016, President François Hollande restored the historic name of Garde Nationale for the volunteer reserve.

Manhattan, had come back to us with an assassin's bullet. The 'we've got our eyes on you, my lad' convinced him that this was no longer a time for carelessness. Wanting nothing less than to cause a scandal, fearing the fatal word immediately tweeted – a gesture of gallantry, a hint of banter – he resigned himself to a tiresome self-control. He had returned from a far country.

Hibernatus reproached himself for exaggerating. 'Aren't I become a bit of an arse-licker?' he occasionally wondered. But if you've lost your touch, there's catching up to be done. Something he did by buying the complete works of Tocqueville at Gibert's. He was not far from learning by heart some passages from *Democracy in America*, a topical work published in 1835. It was just unfortunate that shortly after, while arranging his library, he fell upon a little book dedicated to him by one of his former friends, the Tunisian Albert Memmi, *Portrait du colonisé*. He opened it at random: 'The colonized have been told that their music is caterwauling, their painting sugary. They repeat that their music is vulgar and their painting disgusting.' Here is a trap to be avoided, Hibernatus thought. He felt a conflict of duty coming to a head. To be absolutely modern, indeed, that is what Rimbaud had said. But without grovelling. He wanted to have his cake and eat it too. Hence his worries.

This discomfort chimed with that of a country itself torn between a vaguely shameful nostalgia and a need for rejuvenation. The result was an identity not so much unhappy as flocculent. To see more clearly in the confusion that he felt (a state that the rationalist in him reproached), he referred to a book precisely titled *Le Trouble*, by his former philosophy professor François Dagognet. 'Disturbance generally arises from the invasion of a foreign body. The river water muddies when the riverbed is stirred, as its sand and sediment rise up and spoil its limpidity.' This body certainly had nothing Arabic, Malay or Aztec about it, but could one speak of invasion? He had met free spirits, leafed through an uncensored press, and seen adolescents holding candles in great noisy meetings that brought him to ecstasy, without the least external constraint or apparent brainwashing. No cause to cry violation or catastrophe. Transparency and limpidity, moreover, were not values dear to Hibernatus's heart. He had always appreciated the productive character of imbroglios and colloids, the promise of rainbows, the happiness of baroque recomposition and tumult. A bad customer for *La Terre et Les Morts*.[14] Sobered by the perspective of an endless awkward position, a crazy idea sprang to his mind.

'What if I were to actually go there, given that everything here is like America?' Hibernatus said to himself. 'Let's be radical, go to the root. Their present is our future. Has it always been so? Well, I'll learn our future from the horse's mouth.' It had not escaped him, as a new Inspector Columbo, that even if the Conseil Constitutionnel was not yet the Supreme Court, a state of law that steadily raised the judge above the legislator was not an accidental occurrence; that the opportunities offered interest groups to undertake legal actions, or the head of state to show off his lady to the photographers, with the Élysée turned into *Gala* magazine and the bedroom tucked into the office, as well as directly addressing the two houses of parliament before the TV cameras (instead of passing via the president of the Assemblée Nationale, as stipulated by article 18 of the Constitution); that so-called gender theory, the replacement of the Louis XIV chair by the Plexiglas lectern for press conferences, the notion of the presidential 'ticket', and many other novelties celebrated in his native land during his absence, were so many replays of class actions, of the State of the Union address, of gender studies, and so on. He was dawdling; he would make up the time. He would no longer have to run

---

14 A reference to Maurice Barrès's nationalist manifesto.

rather haggardly after the indispensable reforms, eternal half-and-half, perpetual dimwit, shameful hypo booed by the hypers. On his return he would open a 'consulting' office, called *France for Ever*, with a weekly diary on a 'pure play' news site, and the feedback would be explosive. Promoted trendsetter for a backward population, he would lash the moaners and attract under his initials the impatient ones in a hurry to move up the line.

This brilliant idea set his mind racing. He would not lay claim to the White House, but he already saw himself on the way to familiarity with senators, hobnobbing with Bill Gates, sipping a Diet Coke with Schwarzenegger, listening to a lecture by Gorbachev in a Las Vegas casino, conversing with members of the Supreme Court, strolling down Wall Street, visiting the MIT Medialab or AIPAC, the Israel support lobby, to discover everything about the organization of electoral campaigns, and learning about the jurisprudence of sects at the headquarters of the Church of Scientology.

The gap between theory and practice still had to be bridged, which is never that easy for a Frenchman (progressing from invention to industrial patent has never been our strong point). Hibernatus, as we know, was not born yesterday. Used to getting by, like any creature that scribbles away – 'but has no historical consequences in great circumstances, any more than he has ever had in others' (de Gaulle) – he even attributed himself a certain talent for intrigue. That is characteristic of the French, to overestimate their talents.

An acquaintance of his, the founder of a startup in cookware, set him in the right direction. Operating on eBay (secured by PayPal, the fourth largest e-commerce site in France), this future-oriented company seeking a truly collaborative mode of management had abandoned its departures in rafting, karting, paintball and bowling for 'Gatsby evenings', moments of conviviality more propitious to 'team building' (generating shared memories and enabling employees to get to know one another). He had asked for a launching 'speech', and Hibernatus had faxed him some striking elements of language: 'Shift the goalposts, give strong signs, aim at zero risk, show yourself as innovator and citizen, promote alternative solutions, fill the gap, be a leader in the market and aim to be present at the next Consumer Electronics Show in Las Vegas.' The boldness of this proposal had hit the mark, and the venture capitalist spoke to him one day of the 'young leaders' trained by the French American Foundation, unknown to the general public. When he had listed for Hibernatus the star products of this nursery, in other words, everything that had a name in France, left and right together (presidency, parliament, administration, publishing, television, press, industry), this name dropping flabbergasted him. When he suggested pleading his cause with this fabulous recycling and start-up school, Hibernatus saw the heavens open. Two weeks later, however, his friend came back to him in embarrassment: Hibernatus, despite a girlish complexion that no longer deceived anyone, was too old, and no career perspectives could be envisaged for him.

Since this turn to the right had failed, the ambidextrous Hibernatus turned to the left. He approached an old university friend he valued, a dyed-in-the-wool Marxist who had become the organic intellectual of the most avant-garde North American campuses. Could he open a door for him? The other declined rather brusquely. He saw Hibernatus as too soft, politically doubtful, neither for nor against the great Cultural Revolution. Not exactly a social-traitor, but soft wax. Pale pink. It would be compromising for the prospective godfather.

Tired of the struggle, Hibernatus resigned himself to following the democratic path: a regular visa demand at the consulate. He went to deposit his application on avenue Gabriel, complete with name, photos and required details, and waited. One week, two, three. Nothing. Until the day that he found his application in the letterbox. 'Return to sender' – it had not even been opened.

Hibernatus was seriously depressed. He had understood that he would remain on the platform the rest of his life.

An attempt at chronology

The Americanization of the globe, of which Simone Weil had a brilliant presentiment in 1943, is a captivating and decisive process. This is precisely what makes it hard to map. It is no accident that, decisive and captivating as Romanization was, it remains the poor relation of classical studies. First of all, because it is apogees that attract the gaze more than perigees. The bibliography on the century of Augustus is endless, that on Julian the Faithful, otherwise known as the Apostate, is meagre indeed. Then, because a process of this kind is not recorded in the annals, it's periodization is difficult, due to the fact that it is not yet complete, and that the 'soft imprint' offers less of a hold for recording than the 'strong imprint' left by the Roman legions on the territories they occupied. Here we have such clear milestones as the sack of Rome by Alaric (410), the fall of Constantinople (1453), the taking of Tenochtitlan (1521). An evolution of mentalities over several decades is as little conducive to chronology as a change in the climate over several millennia. The result however is here before our eyes. Since the owl of Minerva flies only at dusk, it is only the end of the Atlantic age that will place the caesura where it should be. If we were still living in the Faustian phase of our modernity, we might have noted, in the year of our Lord 1336, Petrach's *Ascent of Mont Ventoux* – marking the entry into a world in which mountains are no longer to be contemplated, like Olympus in ancient Greece, but rather to be conquered. And only when the Roman Empire had disappeared was it possible to distinguish its stages and pivotal moments. All the easier, since hard traces remained, in the provinces as well as the forum. The seven-hilled city aided our work by monumentalizing its globalization in the form of columns and temples, as well as celebrating its conquering generals with a triumph, an official honour widely commented on in writing, granted by the Senate at the conclusion of a 'just' war (when 5,000 enemies, a minimum figure, would be killed by order of the commander-in-chief, consul or emperor). Nothing of the kind in Frisco or Los Angeles, where the broadcasting of emotive and fascinating sound waves leaves no impression in stone. Here we have a nonchalant proselytism, which deprives the archaeology of the present of good documentary sources.

The immediate history that anatomizes prematurely is always dangerous, and I am not a historian. Besides the fact that gentle slopes do not have warning signs, the risk would be, as always, to be magnetized by events. The establishment of Disneyland Paris, which provoked loud outcries and was seen as a 'cultural Chernobyl', was an event of lesser import than the slow shift of artistic hegemony from Paris to New York. But when did what has been called the 'theft of contemporary art' begin? 1915? 1920? 1947? It burst to light at Venice in 1964, but this was only an arrival point. And when did drum majorettes first appear in the village square, with their staffs and red busbies? The reversed baseball cap in Clichy-sous-Bois? The 'life and well-being' section in bookshops where the human sciences had reigned supreme? The use of first names in classrooms and the familiar *'tu'* on TV shows? This latter might derive from the English 'you', and be prevalent across the Channel, but its imperative use reached us from across the Atlantic, from where it first took hold of our 'showbiz', then of our political personnel (taken over by 'celebs', in the way that Monsieur Le Trouhadec was taken over by debauchery).[15] Beginnings and ends are somewhat arbitrary. At what date, for example, did literary studies cease to have social utility? There is no doubt about this in our universities, among either professors or students (nowadays female), but no decree ever decided the matter. We need also take account of arbitrariness and individual affinities, which do not respect the rhythm of the seasons. The champions of 'national independence' see the de Gaulle years 1958–69 as an Indian summer, the Mitterrand intermezzo of 1981–83 as a sign of spring, and Chirac's 'no' to the Iraq invasion of 2003 as a ray of sunshine in midwinter. For supporters of the 'Western alliance', on the other hand, it is de Gaulle who represents winter and Mitterrand autumn, while Chirac's veto was a cold spell going against the grain. There is no accounting for tastes.

The chronogram given below by way of aperitif is partly a game. It is an invitation to the reader to propose others, as each person will have their own compass and agenda. Strong signals and weak signs are interposed, for which I apologize. What remains when everything has been forgotten is more in the way of *West Side Story* or the fishnet stockings of Cyd Charisse than Richard Nixon's abandoning the gold standard or Georges Marchais's abandoning the dictatorship of the proletariat on behalf of the French Communist Party. Memory itself makes a selection between what is serious and what is not. I simply note that the words and music of Stephen Sondheim and Leonard Bernstein (1961) have survived the 106 proposals of the *Programme Commun* (1981). Culture has no respect for chronological order.

My particular bullet points, on grounds of incompetence, are drawn only from France. And the sequence chosen, the

---

15 A reference to a celebrated play of 1923 by Jules Romains, *Monsieur Le Trouhadec saisi par le débauche*.

short twentieth century, which begins just after the bloodshed of the Great War (1,700,000 dead in our own ranks, plus 4,000,000 wounded and invalid), is arbitrary enough. For the British, the same exercise would have to begin in 1945 (and for the British Empire in 1942, with the fall of Singapore). With the passing of time, France overtook Great Britain, but for both countries, the war acted as a trigger. What began the ongoing descent from the podium was respectively a false military victory (1918) and a genuine but exhausting victory (1945). '*Polemos* is the father of all things' (Heraclitus) – the best as well as the worst.

1919. Versailles treaty. For the first time in two centuries, the French text of an international agreement is not the agreed one. President Wilson demands a version in English. French ceases to be the language of diplomacy.

1920. Foundation in New York, by Katherine Dreier, Marcel Duchamp and Man Ray, of the Société Anonyme, a venue for exhibiting modern art. 'The most intelligent man of this first half of the twentieth century, and for many people the most disturbing' (André Breton on Duchamp) had settled in the United States in 1915. The urinal signed R. Mutt, Duchamp's famous ready-made, was exhibited in New York in 1917 (behind a screen).

1925. Metro-Goldwyn-Mayer acquires Crédit Commercial de France's shares in the film company Gaumont. Confirmation of the transfer of the dream factory from Paris to Hollywood.

1926. Charles Pathé transfers to Kodak the monopoly on the manufacture of celluloid film, which he had obtained from George Eastman before the war.

1927. Warner Bros. produces the first talking picture, *The Jazz Singer*. 'If it works', said the producer, 'the whole world will speak English.' (Sound film would only reach France in 1930.)

1943. Creation of AMGOT (Allied Military Government of Occupied Territories). Confusing liberation with occupation, President Franklin Roosevelt signs a project for the administration of liberated France that would give the supreme Allied command full authority over the entire territory, envisaging a currency printed in the United States and distributed to the French population by the American administration. In spring 1944 de Gaulle successfully thwarts this plan, with the support of General Dwight Eisenhower.

1946. Signature of the Blum-Byrnes agreement. Vichy had prohibited American films. A portion of the French debt is wiped out, in exchange for which the United States, following the perspicacious maxim that 'trade follows the film', demands dropping the quota on American productions and a major reduction in exclusive runs for French films (from seven to four weeks). In reaction to this, a committee in defence of French cinema is formed (Jean Marais and Simone Signoret), and the Centre National du Cinéma comes to the aid of French films, whose production has fallen by half. (In Germany after the war there is no restriction on the distribution of American films.)

1946. In parallel with the Marshall Plan, the United States launches the Fulbright programme – for the intellectual reconstruction of the West.

1948. Promulgation of the Universal Declaration of Human Rights, 'the moral horizon of our time'. Voted on by the UN General Assembly meeting in Paris, at the Palais de Chaillot, but drawn up at Lake Success, New York, in 1947 under the aegis of the great Eleanor Roosevelt, the late president's widow, this represented in two respects a considerable advance on the French declaration of 1789. It was the individual as such, whether stateless, refugee, migrant or asylum seeker, who became the subject of inalienable rights, and the principles laid down, though not obligatory, imposed themselves on all countries. René Cassin obtained agreement that the first sentence of the declaration should take over the first article of the French declaration, with 'man' replaced by 'human beings', who 'are born free and equal in dignity and rights'. The 'and of the citizen' disappeared. In the mind of the Enlightenment, this had referred civil rights to the existence of a citizenship that gave itself its own laws, whereas in the United States man obtained his rights from God, his creator (including the right to carry weapons at school, by virtue of the Second Amendment). Though the Supreme Being was absent from the preamble, religion is frequently mentioned.

1950. The Congress for Cultural Freedom is held in Paris.

1953. Foundation of *L'Express* by Jean-Jacques Servan-Schreiber and Françoise Giroud, which would become in 1964 the first French news magazine, after the model of *Time*.

1955. Establishment of Europe 1, the first private radio station.

1956. First surfers at Biarritz.

1959. First bestseller list in a French weekly.

1959. Launch of the radio programme *Salut les copains*. Appearance of the 45-rpm record, invented in the United States in 1949, and the use of the familiar '*tu*' between presenters and interviewees. Inspired by Elvis Presley and the British Teddy Boys, the new singing idols Johnny Hallyday (Jean-Philippe Smet), Eddy Mitchell (Claude Moine), Sylvie Vartan, Dick Rivers (Hervé Forneri) and Frank Alamo (Jean-François Grandin) forge a counter-culture (with a French nuance in the form of Françoise Hardy). This represented the full emergence of a new age group, adolescents, whose star programme '*Vous êtes formidables*' opened on a theme taken from the New World Symphony.

1963 (22 June). '*La folle nuit*', a free concert on the place de la Nation in Paris. 'What we glimpse here is the future', notes Edgar Morin (with his usual lynx eye). The start of merchandizing, fan clubs, and industrial showbiz. *Zazou* becomes *yéyé*,[16] 'I'm *swing*' becomes 'I'm *rock*'. Increase in sound volume and qualitative leap.

1964. Rauschenberg receives the Grand Prize of the Venice Biennale. The end of the École de Paris, a city whose longstanding central position in the art world now becomes peripheral. The new references are Pollock, Newman, Rothko, De Kooning, Kline, Motherwell . . . 'From now on, if he wants to pursue an international career, a European artist has to live or exhibit in New York.' The rise of the New Wave in cinema attenuates and conceals the disappearance of France as the centre of art auctions and the art scene. By 2015, Paris held no more than 4 per cent of the world market in artworks.

1972. At the Cannes festival, the choice of films presented would no longer depend on the minister of foreign affairs, but simply on the organizing committee. This year's jury is headed by the American director Joseph Losey. Since 1946, and for some twenty years, only French writers had held this position. From now on, with the exceptions of Tennessee Williams in 1976, Françoise Sagan in 1979 and William Styron in 1983, cinema would be judged only by cinema people. Despite the opening to films from elsewhere by a remarkable president (Gilles Jacob), the glamour of the red carpet each year transports our shared imaginary and the town of Cannes to California. The assertion of independence of the greatest festival and world market in film coincided with *Independence Day*, finally emancipated from European literary sponsorship. 'Besides, cinema is an industry', André Malraux had warned.

1974. A pivotal year: France Gall and Michel Berger choose to live out their love affair in Los Angeles. And Valéry Giscard

---

16 The *zazous* were a rather dandyish youth subculture reacting to the austerity of the occupation and postwar years. The onomatopoeia '*yéyé*' was applied to the pop music of the 1960s: 'Yeah, yeah, yeah . . .'

d'Estaing (VGE), at the end of a campaign conceived by Joseph Napolitan, an electoral adviser to Kennedy, is elected president. For the first time in France, a candidate enrols his family in his publicity (one of his daughters poses alongside him on an election poster). VGE asks a future great cinéaste, Raymond Depardon, to film his campaign, and an already famous photographer, Jacques-Henri Lartigue, to take the official photo (not a book or a library in sight). His first address is made in English. The programme recedes behind the profile, print behind image, the public behind the private. Casual clothing (lounge suit instead of evening dress), relaxation (a new rhythm for the 'Marseillaise'). The slogan: 'Rejuvenate France' ('1 per cent of the world population').

1981. Candidacy of the clown Coluche for president of the republic. Casting political power into derision is a happy preamble to financial power, in which the contribution of a professional helps a good deal. Soon after, Ronald Reagan gives ideas to Yves Montand. Explosion of free (and soon, commercial) radio stations. Success of *Dallas* and *Dynasty*.

1984. Abolition of the *'thèse d'état'*.[17] Future candidates would be recommended a US-style PhD. Subsequent establishment of the 'LMD' system (*licence, master, doctorat*).

1989. First meeting of the conference *'La Cité de la réussite'*. Business leaders, media heroes and audio-visual stars fill the main amphitheatre of the Sorbonne for two days to celebrate their social success.

1998. Halloween, the day of the dead. Pumpkins, masks and candies swell the supermarket shelves, children ring doorbells, sociologists debate. It is said that this tidal wave comes from America. Later we learn that it is in fact a Celtic ritual, which reached North America via Ireland and Wales. The label makes the fame and success of the eponymous film.

---

17 A superior doctoral dissertation.

1998. Victory of the French football team, known as *black-blanc-beur*,[18] in the World Cup, with the anthem 'We Are the Champions'. By way of the (anti-racist) celebration of black and *beur*, the ethnic principle dominant in America is naturalized in France, replacing the old national principle. The left substitutes diversity for equality. Slippage from the social to the societal. The issue is no longer the exploitation of one class by another, but discrimination against minorities.

1998. Sorbonne Declaration (a year before that of Bologna). Adoption of the graduate and postgraduate model for European higher education. Replacement of the three-term by the semester system (adopted in 2002), and of units of value by credits, the ECTS (European Credit Transfer System): 60 per year, 180 for the *licence* degree. Reason: better international recognition of French courses.

2000. At railway stations and airports, the Relais H newsstands ('H' for Hachette, a firm founded in 1852) become Relay, a change not applied in clinics and hospitals. The French spelling is retained for the dying and handicapped.

2005. Ceremony of degree awards at Sorbonne Universités imitates the desired model: doctoral candidates in black robes, and mortarboards thrown in the air at the end of the exercise. The network of research students, known as Doc'Up, organizes events such as 'After Work', 'Summer Party', and sports matches.

2007 (7 November). Speech to the US Congress by President Nicolas Sarkozy: 'That day [when Americans walked on the Moon] America was universal and each one of us wanted to be part of this great adventure. What was most extraordinary for us was that through your literature, your cinema, your music, it seemed to us that America always seemed to emerge ever greater and stronger from the adversity and the

---

18 'Black-White-Arab', with 'black' significantly appropriated from English.

challenges it faced. And it seemed to us that instead of causing America to engage in self-doubt, these difficulties only strengthened her belief in her values ... And let me say this as I stand before you here in this Congress. America's strength is not only a material strength. It is first and foremost a moral strength, a spiritual strength.'

2009. France rejoins the military committee of NATO, an appendage of the Atlantic Alliance, which it had left in 1966 (the United States provides 50 per cent of NATO's resources and 75 per cent of its military capacity). The 'transatlantic link' is re-established.

2016. Summer Olympics at Rio de Janeiro. For the first time, French is dropped from announcements and speeches as an official language of the games, with no government protest. The editorial offices of the *International Herald Tribune* (the pan-European daily), now *New York Times International Edition*, leave Paris for New York and Hong Kong. In Paris, iTélé is rechristened CNews.

2017. The presidential candidate Emmanuel Macron, former minister for economy and industry, listens to the 'Marseillaise' not with his arms by the side of his body, but in the posture required of American citizens when the national anthem is played: right arm folded, hand on heart. A posture now transgender and universal. The organizers of the French bid for the Olympics adopt as their motto 'Made for sharing'.

This last date is only a frozen frame in a slippage under way, as commonplace as can be, an umpteenth *translatio imperii et studiorum*, as there have been so many times in the past (from Athens to Rome, from Rome to Byzantium, from Byzantium to Venice, from Florence to Paris, and so on). Nothing about it is shocking or even serious. The annals suggest that the title role on the world stage lasts some five centuries or more, before the next in line takes the lead. From the quattrocento to the American century, Western Europe fulfilled its contract and can leave the pole position with its head high. There is no scandal if it is in the process of hanging up the gloves. It will have transmitted the testimony. And if within this civilization that has modestly become once again a culture, France in particular played its part as a 'great power', with highs and lows, for nearly three centuries (1640–1940), this can be seen as an exploit (especially if we grant between fifty and a hundred years for the accepted dominance of a cross-border regency). This does not mean abandoning a place, but changing a function. And often for the better. The fine days of the mind are not those of the balance sheet – a theme to return to.

4

What Is the New Civilization?

There is not and will never be a new man, but our ways of organizing life, and of each person dreaming their own life, are subject to periodic renovations. The latest in date of these inventions, which believes and presents itself as universal, has modified our values and our customs. The game of living has changed its rules. It has three fetishes: space, image, and happiness. The American formula, like the previous ones, has its costs and its advantages. A provisional balance-sheet can be proposed.

Breathing the same atmospheric layer beneath the same heavenly dome, traversing the same planet with the same nervous cabling, same skeleton and same organs, it is hard to see how the human mammal could have fundamentally changed its concerns since it first stood up on two feet with its toes finally parallel (no longer with the opposable big toe which delayed the landfall of the tree-dwelling primates). The foot on the ground was very likely its most decisive step. Vertical posture freed the hands for the making of tools, the mouth for articulated speech, and increased the endocranial capacity. Environment, microbes and climate then took charge of allocating agendas as a function of wild animals, firearms and tools, once the art of cracking nuts with stones had ceased to satisfy.

The reindeer civilization of the Lapps is not that of the Perigordian bison, the Bronze Age produces a different one from the Stone Age, and a civilization based on rice is not the same as one based on maize. All the same, however, every member of our species, in the hundred thousand years that we have been burying our dead and leaving offerings in their tombs, has had to struggle, and will continue to struggle, with space, time, desire, death and signs. The points to negotiate are invariant, despite the relationships between them shifting according to the selective pressures of the environment. The same is true of genetics. 'Starting from a tiny alphabet of genes, the environment can write a thousand different books' (Boris Cyrulnik). The same musical notes can produce Monteverdi or Wagner; the same fabric can produce the Bayeux tapestry, a Gobelin or a Jean Lurçat. Each civilization invents its particular combination, but if the weft was not the same in the Corrèze as in Zimbabwe, humanity would not be one, and its various combinations would rub shoulders in space like foreign species. They would be unable to influence, affect or exasperate one another if they did not share the same pack of cards. If they do not play on the same keys, or in the same key, even if they do not equally solicit the same tendencies or impulses, each has its own truth and all have something essential to tell us, not only about themselves, but about us. We could not understand Taoism or practise the techniques of Chinese meditation if China were nothing more than a territory or a culture, a region of the universal soul. No Westerner could convert to Islam by reciting his Al-Fatiha if Islamic civilization did not generate in them certain affinities, or make up for something lacking. Virtually, there is a Chinese and a Muslim in each of us, and this is a score that any of us may play, as witness the number of conversions.

Similarly, we would not extend such a welcome to Americanism, in Europe and elsewhere, we would not make it a social obligation to 'save the date' instead of *'retenez la date'*, a political obligation to present ourselves for election with wife and children instead of presenting a programme, or a diplomatic obligation to immediately 'punish' or bomb a country that displeases us rather than seek a dialogue with them before 'striking' – in short, we would not have changed our ways of being in the world, or of making war, if we did not have serious predispositions within us. No one is born 'American' from head to toe, but anyone can become this, with greater or lesser facility. And it is very likely easier for an Irish, Italian or Greek to become naturalized or integrated, liberating what was virtually American in their mind, than for a Chinese, an Indian or a Bantu. The natives of Europe have an advantage, by having in their genetic or rather genealogical baggage certain elements ready for use – the Old and New Testaments, the Latin alphabet, linear time, the syllogism and Galileo – all of which would be rather less useful for them in China. These acquisitions facilitate their acclimatization or recycling across the Atlantic, as shown by our geeks, computer engineers and technicians who do very well in New York or California. A native-born American is certainly more predisposed to Americanism than someone contracted or co-opted, but it is still possible to have spent one's childhood and youth in Rome, Madrid or Paris and still have every chance of ascent to the American paradise. No one should despair.

It follows from this that a value judgement as to the comparative merits of this or that formula for managing existence can never be more than a judgement of mood or opportunity, depending on our habits and attachments. Everything is relative, and we should refrain from laying down absolutes, all the more so as each variation of the anthropological invariant has its drawbacks as well as its advantages, and none of them is totally foreign to us. We judge ourselves by judging others. But what is favourable to one person, in the milieu of their incubation, can turn out damaging to the survival of another once transferred out of its own sphere. The microbes to which Europeans had become immune by the sixteenth century killed the Amerindians, and cultural traits that are healthy for an American may prove pathological in a European.

The succession of peoples on the bridge of humanity's flagship shifts the balance in the original situation as well as the hierarchy previously prevalent. The outgoing teams tend most often to adopt the priorities of the latest arrivals, if only to remain on board. It goes without saying that America is energy, force flow, creative whirlwind, élan vital. 'Destructive of immobility and constructive of the future' (Élie Faure). God is American, merciless and muscled. It is logical that the excluded or unfortunate who wish to remain in the game go there to get fresh ideas and polish up their act. But Americanism, an ideology without saying so, and despite the word having been abused by pre-war reactionaries, has also the virtue of indicating the primacy of space over time, of image over writing, and of happiness over the drama of living. Or again, of the external over the internal, of the seen over the read, and of the love of answers over the love of questions. Three small changes of emphasis that, while seeming slight, have shifted the inner substance of our being in the world.

This new psychic economy has an element: space; a regime: the image; and a fixed star: happiness.

We shall examine each in turn, even if these three priorities all fit together (catalysed in the slogan 'America First').

Space above all

If Europe is rooted in time, America is rooted in space. This original pact undoubtedly constitutes its spiritual principle, just as time does for Europe. This is not a metaphysical point but a geophysical one (and Hippolyte Taine, not so old hat after all, saw the importance of this genetic selection of mentalities by environment). 'The history of a people', said the geographer Paul Vidal de La Blache, 'is inseparable from the land it inhabits'; you do not choose the place where you are born, and it leads you to see the world through its distorting glasses. On this side of the ocean, there is little accumulated space and too much time. On the other side, much space and little time, where the clocks started running more recently (almost no Palaeolithic art). In Europe, a crammed place where a neighbour was for a long time a danger, it was not so easy to find a comfortable spot. In America, an immense land and not an anxious one, it was always possible to seek a place further on, west of the Appalachians, where there was land in abundance for the immigrants arriving from Europe: Irish, German or Scandinavian (65 hectares per family in Lincoln's Homestead Act of 1862). There, civilization meant pushing back the frontier, and the word 'colonist' was a term of praise. Here, a man would feel that much more accomplished if he had rounded off his patch, and 'landlord' was not an insult.

The horizon is sometimes ahead, sometimes within. Ahead, it glows at the end of a limitless and decentred space, available and legendary; within, it plunges into unfathomable 'year zeroes' and misty origins, antedated or fantasized. The physical spaces themselves do not have the same substance. The difference is not only one of scale, between the waterfalls of Niagara and that in the Bois de Boulogne, between the Rockies and the Alps, the Midwest and the Beauce. It is not simply a matter of scale, but one of dynamics. American space is not dwelling but movement. The road is its characteristic symbol. Cart, stagecoach, automobile, motorbike, jet plane, rocket. But always 'Go West, young man.' On horseback or Harley-Davidson, and in lunar module to the moon. From road movie to *Star Wars*. From the biker with chromium and leather boots to the astronaut in his capsule. James Dean, Marlon Brando, Jack Kerouac, Peter Fonda, Cormac McCarthy. Route 66, mobile home,

Myspace. *The Wild Bunch* and *Easy Rider*. The blue ribbon leading straight to nowhere – the frontier always pushed farther back, bringing liberation to whoever crosses it – gives rise to the ideal of mobility in home, career and dreams. Put your home on wheels and leave. Have several lives. This is the gap between terroir and territory, land to work and land to conquer, the plough and the Colt. From the automobile to the locomotive, the American space is hope; if it does not work out here, I can go somewhere else. No forced residence. No unchanging business card. The European home lies rather in expectation: the trajectory from sin to redemption, from ignorance to knowledge, from war to peace. There is also the distinction between nomadic and sedentary, between moving on and dodging, the writer-adventurer in the image of Jack London – sailor, worker, laundry-man, gold-digger, seal-hunter, globetrotter and finally millionaire – and the member of the Institut Français, a single job, a single address, and repeating his work a hundred times. A well-cultivated clearing or a well-fortified village, surrounded by heath, woodland and menacing forests, a mosaic of small closed-in worlds, a rosary of hermitages, a scattering of 'little holes'. Not open land to cross, but niches in which to put down your suitcase and make your nest. Hence two different ways of learning to walk. On this side a road is appreciated for the staging-posts it promises, the pleasure of halting in places signalled or noted in advance, well-known mounds or inspirational hills. Whereas over there, roads mean the intoxication of what lies ahead, and above all, of leaving behind a dead skin, a life one no longer wishes to revisit. Each has its prize for excellence. In terms of publications, *National Geographic* in the New World, history magazines in the Old (in which Vidal de La Blache, in the 'gospel of the Republic', appears as hors d'oeuvre, and Ernest Lavisse as the main course).[1]

---

[1] Respectively the fathers of modern geography and history in France.

The attention that one side pays to outside spaces, the other gives to those inside. The 'little sensation' of the Impressionist is not the great space of Abstract Expressionism – and it is not the size of the canvas that makes the difference, but the splash or concentration of touch. The Expressionist mystique works from the outside in.; the Impressionist mystique follows the opposite course, from inside outward. One is introvert, the other extrovert. James Joyce aimed to discover the world in a nutshell. Barnett Newman, in 1948, had no need for nutshells: 'We are freeing ourselves of the impediments of memory, association, nostalgia, legend, myths, or what have you, that have been the devices of Western European painting.' If there were symbolic crests for such impalpable things, they would oppose in literature Marcel Proust to Walt Whitman, in cinema Luchino Visconti to John Ford, in painting Pierre Bonnard to Pollock (or, in monochrome, Pierre Soulages with his saturated blacks to Rothko with his luminous spaces), and in sculpture, Rodin or Giacometti to Donald Judd or Richard Serra. There is a poetry of externality, which can attain the grandiose; and there is a different poetry of internality, whose grandeur may be inversely proportional to its size and volume. It is possible to love both, and still better not to confuse the two.

Every inhabited space has its special places, but unlike Camus's Tipasa, not all places are inhabited by gods or even phantoms. 'Zones' are without memory, proper name or physiognomy. This is the difference between a quarter and a sector, a city and a conurbation. The niche hollowed out by rubbing and the rectangular space divided up by a plan. Between the organic and the mechanical. On one side, the labyrinthine and centripetal city, with little squares, alleys, shady passageways, twists and turns full of possibilities. On the other, rectilinear and centrifugal, roadways without sidewalks, streets with no name and priority to the flow of traffic. With bungalow estates, the outer reaches of the grid strewn with hypermarkets (France has the European record for these), the storing of time gives way to a spatial functionality that de facto acts against local public services, the municipal crèche or the media library. Gigantic complexes of private leisure and commerce appear, such as the EuropaCity projected in Île-de-France with its Abu Dhabi–style snow park. Crumbs of America in the open countryside, where a Leader Price discount store is surrounded by petrol station, drugstore and gym club. Bungalows, white fences, lawns, the same formula repeated in suburbs and communities. The same 'shoeboxes' in our own faubourgs. The continent of commemorations, where people like to blow out the candles, is modelling itself on the continent of locomotion, where people like to change their vehicle, and if our *lieux-dits*, like the Parisian 'Left Bank' and 'Right Bank', remain places of memory where a certain view of the world prevails (I personally avoid the Right Bank), each agglomeration bears witness to a certain levelling of the 'offices of the mind'. In Paris, for example, the café and the salon seemed to have made peace, whereas, a hundred years ago, they were in a war well related by Léon Daudet, a great friend of Proust, who dedicated to him *The Guermantes Way*:

> The café boor presents himself in a less polished, soaped and pomaded aspect than the salon boor. He keeps his angles, his gleam and his points; he is often heard to say, like the triumphant Roman: 'You are a boor.' True spirit is required in the café, and immediately repaid in the form of resounding laughter, whereas too often the salon spirit is only a sham, a pale imitation, approved, propagated and prolonged by forced and conventional smiles. A false talent gets nowhere in a café, any more than a false coin. In short, the café is the school of frankness and spontaneous

pleasantry, whereas the salon is generally the school of the cliché and imbecile fashion.[2]

Paris has kept its cafés and closed its salons, but under different signboards the squabble between niches continues, each clinging to the narcissism of little differences, which is precisely their charm. These differences are pursued for other social reasons, as sociologists of distinction such as Pierre Bourdieu like to recall when they contrast academic society with media society. Places, from the very fact that they are the product of history, can be said to be 'dated', but even when destroyed or deserted, they leave a kind of digital imprint in our cities and our minds.

Anti-places leave no imprint. They can disfigure but not configure. Movable, interchangeable and replicable at will, petrol stations, freeway tollbooths, motels, supermarkets, car parks, airports and stations have no signature or even anything to identify them. But this lack of spirit is also a spirit, that of a no man's land hard-pressed to become a territory, for example by giving places proper names (in the United States, the names of cities are repeated from state to state, which is precisely why the state has to be made clear after the name). The anti-place moves to wherever it sees fit. It is not stubborn. If it sees a more profitable opportunity elsewhere, that is where it goes. That is its democratic and well-behaved side. High places, however, do not have this flexibility. They deem themselves irreplaceable, unshiftable, and stand by their pedigree. That is what presses châteaux, the dwellings of famous people, grand houses, sites inscribed in the national heritage, to cling on and persist. The supreme thought of a place is to transmit itself. To descendants, to the city, to the region or the state. And not to communicate.

What does communication mean? To transport information *through space*. What does transmission mean? To

---

2   Léon Daudet, *Salons et journaux*, 1917.

transport information *through time*. Communication has eroded, harassed, and finally swallowed up transmission, as the spirit of America has that of Europe. It is no surprise that the most communicative of civilizations has brought the art and techniques of communication to an apogee. What is more surprising is that we ourselves practise the forward flight from transmission into communication – in education, the state, museums, churches and professional training. Screens thumb their noses at the school, as the journalist does to the professor, the tubes to the tutor, and the smartphone to the grandfather. Where have our communication machines come from in almost a century? From a formidable laboratory-country that invents and perfects them from one year to the next. And space, with the aid of these prodigies, has taken time in its folds and subjected a dreamy civilization to the chronometry of the man in a hurry: 'We don't have time, shorten it please, we have to go on air.' Our time is nibbled away, whereas space is no longer measured. The *speedé* [= hyper] of the 2000s, who phones, clicks, plugs in, switches on and off and jumps from one plane to another, divides his diary into fifteen-minute slots and his time-code into seconds, but his zone of useful movement stretches over thousands of kilometres. The villager of 1900, who went to mass or the town hall on foot, or from his farm to the departmental capital on horseback, proceeded the other way round. He inscribed his days in a time measured in seasons and generations, but in a space measured in steps and miles. In the blink of an eye, a single century, that separating the bicycle chain from the diesel engine, distances have become unimportant to us, but the slightest delay becomes intolerable. Globalization has gone together with de-historicization; as if, to the extent that our networks and freeways (terrestrial, aerial and informational) have extended, chronologies have contracted. And our motors move faster than our reflexes. Hence the inversion of precedence in the family.

Daddy asks the kids to teach him how this works. The kids do not ask anything in return, except cash to buy the latest video game or play eSports on their console (several hundred million participants globally, vocabulary completely in English). Techniques of effective communication have left the arts of effective transmission far behind. For YouTubers and millennials, the American speciality has supplanted European originality even in Europe itself.

How has this happened? By replacing institution by equipment. Institutions make a bridge between yesterday and today; equipment, between here and there. The former have a function (family, church, state, academy, school, language) and guarantee transmission, while the second has a circulation. The explosion of mobility (of persons, capital, opinions, skills, jobs, and so on) has gone hand in hand with the implosion of continuities (and the discomforts of identity that result from this). The infrastructures of space, fostered by digitalization, have eclipsed those of time. What is not rechristened 'space' today? An automobile, a theatre, a waiting room ... Our streets are reclassified as 'pedestrian spaces', churches as 'spiritual spaces', playgrounds as 'children's spaces', meeting-rooms as 'spaces of exchange and dialogue', the SNCF [France's state-owned railway company] as a 'co-working space', and the forest of Brocéliande as a 'green space'. We find it easy to insert the local into the national, and the national into the global, like Russian dolls. We find it harder to insert one age of life into a whole life. We forget the dates of birth of our parents, and where our grandparents are buried (if they were not incinerated); but we have GPS (and soon, Galileo) on our dashboard. Our position in time is misty, but in space we know where we are within four metres. Localizing is easy, periodizing hard. 'Where are you?' is our first question on the smartphone. 'Where do you come from?' would be out of place. And we tacitly ask our screens, day after day, to present to us a newly remade world that has arisen from nothing. If not, I zap, and zapping means cutting off what endures. Like the market economy or something that flares up in the morning and dies in the evening, for no apparent reason.

Machines to domesticate time have a handicap: repetition. They do not change their *look* each year. That is their merit, which harms them. When they do not suffocate, they make people yawn. Always the same! In contrast, our apparatuses for domesticating space are renewed every day, and each new model of smartphone makes us forget the old and anticipate the next. We forget the way of being both *today and yesterday*: by approaching the altar or the trade union building, by learning Latin or the words of the 'Internationale', by reciting Valéry's 'La Cimetière marin' in school, singing the 'Marseillaise' or 'Veni Creator'; but the prostheses that allow us to be both *here and elsewhere* – computers, laptops, fibre optics, FaceTime – replace these so well that we are no longer aware of their existence, unless we find ourselves not in two times at once, but in two places. And the farther away are the dead, the closer are the distant. The work of mourning is eclipsed, but I can speak face-to-face with anyone calling me from 10,000 kilometres away. And if the flesh of Jesus Christ, who died 2,000 years ago, is teleported by the host to the tongue of the communicant, faith is needed to enjoy this chronological short circuit. The remote presences brought to us by our devices, open to atheists and baptised alike, are easier to access. Hence the success. We are a society of access.

Here we are then in a regime of space. With politicians for whom movement is good in itself, no matter in what direction – '*En marche!*' With business managers who transform the old individual office into a Flexi-Desk, an open space with no accredited place, a question of ambience. Working space no longer has door or dividers. Economists no longer calculate the gross national product, which accounted for the production of the citizens of a country, within and outside its borders, but the gross domestic product, that of the territory. Our professional appraisers and art critics, who used to validate and assess a work in terms of time, practise for contemporary art a validation by space: what counts is not that a work 'holds up', but that it is exhibited and quoted at the same moment in Düsseldorf, London, New York and Shanghai. Its years will be numbered, but it will be everywhere. And since the least immobility is seen as an injury to life, our superiors abandon the seated position, the classic sign of authority – that of Christ in majesty on the abbatial tympanum – to arrive with a supple and determined leap, like a dynamic young president, at the Plexiglas lectern for the weekly press conference. General acceleration of tempo, from rapidity of speech (young people talk very quickly) to shots in a film ('choppy' editing), to meetings in a diary ('I'm ultra *booké*'), to the latest smartphones ('Have you got the new one?'). We precipitate the moment and jump from one country or subject to another. Roller skates, boards and scooters, from seven to seventy-seven years old. Surfing, sliding and fluidity. Contagious fidgeting: 'Move yourself, Europe.' Priority of just-in-time and stock rotation. Burn out at the end of the roll.

Americans know how to move and dance like no one else. Obama as much as Fred Astaire and Gene Kelly. And the step is all the quicker when memory is lighter. The American nation was built up by constantly renewing itself so as to forget and lighten the burden of the past. Europe has done the opposite. It has constructed its modernity by reinjecting a long history into its present: the Carolingians resurrected the Roman purple, the Italian Renaissance the golden section, the French Revolution returned to the toga and buskin, and German romanticism exalted the Gothic when it was still fresh from the mould. This made for two different models of development. The one believes humanity has a common destiny because it has a history in common, the other because it has a planet in common. Neither Vico nor Hegel would find a place in New York – 'new', for them, meaning poor and superficial. And if the immense land of Brazil took Auguste Comte, creator of the 'religion of humanity', as its mentor, this was in all likelihood to compensate for the disturbing thought of too much space with the assurance of an exceptional depth of time (the Positivist calendar).

Each civilization has a necessary ambivalence, a kind of double bookkeeping, and its faith in space has given America its finest victories. The 'new frontier' (the old one came to an end around 1890) took it to the moon, and interplanetary conquest happily extended that of the Far West (bringing more goods and fewer deaths). Since *having* takes place in space, and *being* in time, the spatial presses towards a completion of what has been acquired by adding more to it, and the patina of time presses towards deepening what is already there, fold upon fold, touching up at home, lace in the bedroom, history on history, painting on painting, literature on literature – all to the second degree, in an Alexandrian mode, just as Hellenistic culture duplicated and complicated the Hellenic. There is no civilization without its perverse effects. The new one has its liabilities, which do not invalidate it, but which it is good to bear in mind.

First of all, the mistake about connection. This could well be the illusion of the new century (each has its own). To be specific, the confusion between planetary and solidary, uniform and universal. Satellite connections do not by themselves guarantee the sentiment of a common destiny or a duty of solidarity. A humanity lacking memory and project condemns itself, and is soon reduced to the ever more precarious management of its ethnic, religious or political differences. It is not free clicks on the Internet or connected cameras that make 'the species into a single people', but rather the presence among us of what is not seen and cannot be seen. Humanity is fragmented in and by space, but unified in and by time; a species that entrusted its fate to space alone would quite rapidly become a zoo, with a licence for the rich to come and photograph the poor in their reservations. And we know that tourism, the largest industry worldwide, has not particularly favoured the union of hearts and minds.

A model of life, moreover, that makes 'reacting' a prime quality, and that everywhere seeks to gain place so as not to lose time (time is money), can in the long run only brutalize human relations, whether civil or amorous. It short-circuits the protocols and procedures elaborated at great cost over millennia in order to control or delay the beast's assault on its prey, to negotiate impulse and articulate onomatopoeia. To give candidates in a presidential election one and a half minutes each to explain their conception of France and the world amounts to a demeaning akin to an *assault on the security of the European mind*. That this speed dating, preceded by mocking sketches amounting to the grotesque, can be accepted without flinching by politicians, says much on the degree of *de-civilization* (or normalization) that our acclimatized, or rather alienated, forum has reached. When time is lacking, the tone rises and the level falls. Likewise in the papers, where fear of boring puts a long speech into a side box and a headline is designed to hit like a fist, where concision becomes excess and brevity becomes idiocy. No chance. The more complex the world becomes, the more it must be made simple. Complexity has its cost, but simplicity pulls the strings, and diplomacy in 140 characters is becoming a must. The greater the need for rationality, and thus for consistency and continuity, the more we are delivered to the intermittencies of tweets and speed watching. The technologies and disciplines of nuance may have disappeared, but if Europeans make American countdowns and timeouts their own, we cannot see how, without pressing the pause button, Europe can avoid entering the age where anything goes, while flattering itself to have joined the twenty-first century.

In a so-called access society, access to truth will become impossibly expensive.

A further perverse effect, and a deadly one: when the historicity of the human condition is denied, a conjunctural and media-driven geopolitics is established, both unrealistic and irresponsible, and set for failure. The latest slogan of the Anglo-Saxon generals is 'war among populations'. This simple phrase alone is enough to predict a disaster. A 'population' – a term from administrative language – denotes 'the set of individuals who inhabit a space'. A people, all those who share the same history, is a population fashioned by time. They owe to time their language, their religion, their eating habits, a way of dressing, and generally, accompanying these distinctive features, a certain pride, a sentiment exasperated by the prolonged presence of intruders on a soil that is not their own. Populations would be far more manageable if they were not constituted into peoples, or at least into long-established tribes, clans and communities. Western parachutists, as they pass through, may well hand out sweets to children, open dispensaries, come to the aid of bullied women and pay local collaborators, but their firepower can do nothing against this long patience. Peoples have time. Neither a precise calendar nor a deadline. The foreigners will have to leave sooner or later. The indigenous will be always here, in their land, with their cousins. The 'Americans' do not like land. Their element is space – clouds and fleets. They have mastery of this (the indigenous have neither fleet nor aviation). The blue of the planet belongs to them. That suits them well: there are neither peoples nor time in the blue.

The element of the indigenous is grey. The armies of the democracies do not like landfall, and this is understandable. That is where things get complicated, where time takes back the upper hand – a history that is not theirs, and of which their leaders have not the slightest idea, having forgotten to consult ethnographers, who indeed know a bit about this, but, having neither shopfront nor coverage in the media, lack existence in the eyes of the decision makers. The land is called Iraq, Afghanistan, Libya. Formerly it was Vietnam, Algeria, Egypt. On each occasion it is space without time.

What won the moon for America, on its way to the planet Mars, has made it lose all the wars it has waged on land for the last half century. The cosmos is worth the loss of a few hilltops. We Europeans, as good and loyal allies, have not gone to the moon, but we have lost the same wars alongside our leader, with the same methods and the same illusions. It is not a win-win situation.

Image above all

America entered history and our hearts through the image; it has optical fibre. Europe entered history and our brains through writing; it has logical fibre. The heroes of the New World smell of neither ink nor turpentine. They are on film. Buffalo Bill did not distinguish himself by his autobiography, but by his exhibitions. We are not familiar with political essays signed by Franklin Roosevelt. President Kennedy left little in the way of diaries or correspondence, not to speak of his successors. Take from de Gaulle his *War Memoirs*, or from Napoleon his *Mémorial de Sainte-Hélène*, and the myth would be incomplete, the transfiguration clumsy. Take Jean Gabin and Michèle Morgan from the France of the Front Populaire and you cut off a finger. Take John Wayne and Marilyn Monroe from the America of the 'New Frontier' and you cut off the legs.

It would be possible to sum up the American century in an album of a hundred photos (a good third of these being of stars), and twentieth-century Europe in an anthology of a hundred texts (a good third being poems, manifestos or short stories). In the former you would find photos with captions, in the latter texts with illustrations. This may be exaggeration, but it would have been impossible to replace Europe without replacing written culture by visual. The cinema created the United States, for which it is far more than a means of influence. It is the origin of its power. Trump, like Reagan before him, is the sheriff in the film. John Wayne at the controls.

The primacy of drawing over symbol, of print over idea, was initially a technological advance. The emergence of the graphosphere, with printing, coincided with the formation of the European nation-states; that of the videosphere, following the cameras, coincided with the rise of the American imperium. The care and genius of the latter is focused on the image, whose engineering it has captured and perfected, ever since the image was no longer the work of human hand. Joseph Nicéphore Nièpce invented the photograph, the Lumière brothers the cinema, but as is well known, the French can invent but do not do industry. It was in the factories and laboratories of America that the kinetoscope, the nickelodeon, the Folding Pocket Kodak, silver nitrate film, the Vitaphone, colour film, CinemaScope, Steadicam, and so on were conceived and mass produced. It is right and proper that they should receive the profits from what they were able to reproduce and produce with their own hands, before the rest of the world. To be sure, the seen was initially fuelled by the read, and the films of Walt Disney recycled tales from Perrault and Grimm. But the comic strip and the animated cartoon won over hearts, and honour must be paid to the world's greatest producer of images, in both quantity and quality. 'American cinema', said Serge Daney, is a pleonasm. How can you love Hollywood without loving America? Stalin, it seems, managed to do so, being a fan of Westerns. Kim Jong-il likewise. But who loved Stalin or Kim Jong-il?

Perhaps God is not American, but neither is he anti-American, to judge by a providential history of visual capture apparatuses that have spread the epic of space across the whole world, via multiplying media – terrestrial, maritime, aerial and spatial. This has transformed the heroes of each era into icons: photography popularized Lincoln, cinema Lindbergh, television Neil Armstrong. Europe might rightly pride itself on the Enlightenment, but this reached a limited number of readers by typography. The United States chose to take light and send it to the four corners of the globe. The American Civil War was the first photographic conflict (far more so than the Crimean War). A happy land of immigration, a Promised Land whose sublime landscapes with their biblical grandeur struck the eyes of the hungry and persecuted of a narrow Old World. A happy chanson de geste, the preamble to which was a monument of silent cinema, *Birth of a Nation* (D. W. Griffith, 1915), and its epilogue a poetic masterpiece, *Heaven's Gate* (Michael Cimino, 1980). In order to grow and believe in their destiny, other countries needed to pin on their lapel a doctrine, a system or a theology – Luther or Rousseau, Auguste Comte, Marx or Nietzsche ... In this domain, the American republic chose economics. A minimal ideology. It entrusted its marvels not to paper but to photosensitive media, which have the gift of printing on all retinas, including those of the illiterate. The cinema actor has an advantage over the author of books: returning physically, intuitively, on each projection, with the result that they can be celebrated *in absentia* while remaining present on the screen long after their death. An advantage not given to the stage actor, the sculptor or the musician.

The prodigy of the visual – all the more inventive and agile to the extent that any pictorial or academic tradition is lacking – has thus enjoyed two exclusive privileges: first of all, to tell stories to the whole world, without need for translators (*Les Misérables* needs these, but not Charlie Chaplin), and thus move the whole earth, excite it, make it laugh or cry. These stories may be those of its enemies, Sitting Bull, Che

Guevara or Malcolm X – recuperated and aseplicized by large-scale productions, not counting the posters, buttons and T-shirts. It is not the same operators at work, but killing your enemy and making him into an idol soon after is not something that just anyone can do. And then rewriting your own story by replaying on the screen the match lost on the field.

All nations have their share of the inadmissible – heretics burned alive, pogroms and witch-hunts, rapes and lynchings, concentration camps, roundups, colonial wars. The American nation has the ability, thanks to John Ford and John Wayne, to make the genocide of its original inhabitants an exalting adventure, to make Vietnam a festival of heroism, thanks to *Rambo* and Sylvester Stallone, and to make Iraq, via *American Sniper* and Clint Eastwood, a competition at a firing range. The powers of paper are very poor by comparison. Thousands of readers, millions of viewers. Art for the élite, art for the masses. Victor Hugo's 'dismal plain' did not make Waterloo a victory in our eyes, nor did his ' "*Donne-lui tout de même à boire", dit mon père*' [' "Give him a drink at least", my father said', in Hugo's poem 'After the Battle'] make the Dos de Mayo a humanitarian gesture. The government of perceptions over half of the planet is a decisive bonus.

According to an IFOP survey, to the question 'Which nation do you believe contributed most to the defeat of Germany?', 55 per cent of French respondents in 1945 said the USSR, against 15 per cent the United States. The same question in 2004 brought an exactly opposite result. This was the effect of *Saving Private Ryan*: the replacement of the real by perception of the real.

The statistics of known military losses in the Second World War show 53 per cent for the Red Army and 1.4 per cent for the American army; 400,000 Americans were killed, almost all soldiers, against 27 million Soviet dead, over half of whom were civilians. No one was surprised on this side of the world to see Vladimir Putin attend the seventieth anniversary ceremony for the Normandy landings, yet not to see François Hollande in Moscow for the seventieth anniversary of the victory over Nazism, alongside representatives of the other half of the world population (China, India, Brazil, and so on). 'Trade follows the film.' And so does amnesia.

Let us try to escape this by moving towards the past. It was by the compulsory use of writing that pre-Hispanic America passed from the stage of a conquered land, in the sixteenth century, to that of an annexed land in the following centuries. The transition from pictography to alphabetic writing, and from image to page, among peoples without an alphabet who had previously operated just with images, completed and sanctioned the annexation of the Americas by the Spanish Empire. The colonization of the imaginary takes place today in the opposite direction and back to front. It leads us from page to shot. And the transition to digital firms up this process. All this owes nothing to the White House or the Pentagon, but rather to MIT, which has only good intentions. It is a matter of technology, and was already so in the past. Montaigne, 'in the face of so many cities razed, so many nations exterminated, so many millions of people put to the sword', spoke quite correctly of 'mechanical victories'. The conquest of America, in the wake of Christopher Columbus's discovery of 1492, represents the most exemplary and most well-known 'clash of civilizations' (coyly renamed, when the 500th anniversary was celebrated in Seville in 1992, the 'encounter of two worlds'). Pre-Hispanic Mexico housed very developed civilizations – the Olmecs of the Gulf, the Mayas of the Yucatan, the Toltecs of the central plateau, whose heirs were the Aztecs. Their formidable empire was decapitated in a few months by Cortès, 1,200 Spanish soldiers, local auxiliaries, horses and a few guns. The gold rush of the early conquistadores evolved with time (around a century) into a transfer of civilization, Europe now annexing the New World.

This success was not simply due to acts of extreme brutality. The Spaniards carried the day in terms of civilization, by virtue of a crushing advance in terms of media. The pre-Columbians were ignorant of the wheel, draught animals and metallurgy. The sight of a horse, and the detonation of a musket, left them petrified. But above all, they had no alphabetic writing, and could only think, communicate, and represent to themselves the course of things by way of pictograms. By progressively imposing on the conquered Amerindians the lines of the alphabet, the Europeans modified their conception of time, which from having been cyclical now became linear. From this point on, conversion to Christianity became possible. There would now be for the Indians a before and an after, a beginning of the world and an end. The Christian narrative became comprehensible. A transition from one civilization to another – which necessarily retained certain relics of the old. The smartphone that makes photos accessible to all, and their transport via social media from one end of the world to the other at a single click, amounts to a shift in the opposite direction, from the left hemisphere of the brain to the right.

Lettered folk do not like the 'mechanical', still less electronics and robotics. Too accustomed to words ending in 'ism', they have an antipathy to words ending in 'ics' (and to mediology as well, which studies the effect of 'ics' on 'isms'). Hence certain errors of attribution, sometimes bordering on naivety. 'We understand absolutely nothing of modern civilization', wrote Georges Bernanos on his return to France after the war, 'if we do not accept right away that it is a conspiracy against every kind of inner life.' The observation is exact, and even prophetic. But to this desolated Christian who no longer recognized the people of his own country, we are tempted to reply: 'No, dear desperate fellow, it is not a plot, but the mechanical effect of a photosensitive medium that has the capacity to reinvent souls.' The hollow man is a gift of photography, for which whether there is anything inside or not is simply a joke. What it values is the exterior, the physical, the *look*. Inner life, for its part, contributes nothing because it does not show itself. So it is not surprising that, once the videosphere was established, the most photogenic of nations, the most cinematographically powerful (though not the most cinephile), brought the most literary of nations to follow its example. And no more surprising that the latest generations of French politicians are the children of *Captain America*, of the television and the Internet, without which, moreover, nothing would seen or heard. There would be no elected politicians, simply scholars, poets or monks.

Number is softened by image, otherwise the 'cold waters of egoistic calculation' would make everyone run away. Visual emotion, distributed each minute, prevents us from dying of cold. It is the fleshly supplement that digital abstraction has greatest need of. The calculator without the camera, the discount rate without the star (an Ethiopian or Syrian baby in her arms), would be Monaco without a love story, a market hall without a market in dreams, which are a human right. The head of state on an official sales trip to a foreign country must as an imperative visit a kindergarten or refugee camp with his wife, in time for the TV news. The logic of interest would be intolerable without our daily dose of touching and disinterested nobility. A topic deserving more attention is the key role of photography in public action, where no one can make themselves loved without being seen, alone or in a selfie with their partner. Image and morals, in the public mind, feed off one another. What would the humanitarian be without the small screen? Or the Apple brand without Steve Jobs, 'a builder of civilization', who will tomorrow give his name to a Paris street? It is the purgatory of the welfare state that it is unable to appear on a screen. The philanthropist easily moves people, the tax inspector has his work cut out. If you have seen Bill Gates – 'the richest man in the world', 'the benefactor of suffering humanity' – enter a radio studio, you have seen what Hegel saw when Napoleon passed beneath his window in Jena: the world spirit not on horseback, but in shirtsleeves. Nietzsche's 'cold monster', the state, has warmed itself up by becoming flesh. The private sector now sponsors, rather than the law financing. A godsend, given the impoverishment of public authorities, for the dilapidated fountains, abbeys, churches and palaces of our old cities, restored by our emperors of the handbag and the cemetery. Do we not have here the dream team of the age, the economics/morality duo in a single exemplary being? Tax inspector, indeed, but before this, Boy Scout in short trousers; inflexible manager, but afterwards ecological conscience; Rothschild bank, but at the same time, ethical investment fund. Audience measurement plus a dose of morality. Business plan plus Mother Theresa. This hot and cold leads to the highest functions.

In this way, French society has put itself into image mode. A proliferation of promotional narcissism. After the 'clash of images', the 'shock book'. Philosophers used to have students and disciples. They taught in schools and universities. The new ones have fans, a hairdresser at the ready and a stage costume. They have moved from the lecture hall to the television, from the course to the talk show. Politicians used to explain their projects in books that they wrote themselves. Now they have ghost writers to sign rapidly produced works like entrance tickets for the show. There are already those who cut directly to the stand-up, skipping the 'printed' stage. Slogans become 'jingles', governments become 'castings', sayings become 'teasers'. And video cameras even invade radio studios. The reason? Sound is heard better if it is imaged. Tocqueville's chapter on the Age of Enlightenment (*The Ancien Régime and the Revolution*, Book III), under the title 'How Writers Became a Political Power, and the Greatest of All', suggests an update: 'How showbiz is becoming a political power, and the greatest of all'. 'Politics is ideas', noted Albert Thibaudet, literary critic and canny chronicle of politics, in 1932, adding: 'In France, a man of government has to represent an idea.' That would take away the jobs of today's politicos. A politician in the videosphere devotes 80 per cent of their time, if in opposition, to the construction of an image, and if in government, to adjustments of this image. It is a daily task, requiring a staff of at least ten persons (family and office). An idea is as much in place here as a bull in a china shop. As for writing, this has retreated to ever shrinking 'book supplements'. The weeklies of the 1960s, such as *Arts*, *Les Lettres françaises* or *Le Figaro littéraire*, are replaced by *Télérama*. In former times, actors and cineastes were asked about their favourite books, but today authors are asked about their favourite TV series. No one expects Marion Cotillard[3] to show us her *Bibliothèque de la Pléiade* collection, but we would much like Jean d'Ormesson[4] to show us his collection of DVDs. The selfie replaces the autograph, a prominent figure is no longer called a 'legend' (from the Latin *legenda*, 'must be read'), but an 'icon' ('pop and shock', if possible). Instalment novels are reborn as TV series, an inspector general of the ministry of education advises teachers of French to give students for comment only magazine articles signed by well-known names – meaning 'famous for being famous', in other words, seen on television. In a field where novelists and poets used to inspire the visual arts, the 'novelization' department works to transpose films, thrillers and TV series into books, derivative products that still bring a good return, even if for every hundred viewers there will be no more than one or two readers. Our optical palette is enriched, and our intelligence for image syntax has gained in sharpness and rapidity (an explanatory sequence

---

3   The actress who portrayed Édith Piaf in *La Vie en Rose*.
4   Novelist and editor (1925–2017), dean of the Académie française.

that needed five minutes in a film can today be cut down to thirty seconds). A good point is exchanged for a restricted vocabulary and a certain incomprehension of a text's unsaid implications and ambiguities. The primacy of oral expression, soon reinforced by the vocal assistance of digital prostheses, will give writings without illustrations the solemnity, both opaque and off-putting, attached to Carolingian antiphonaries and treatises. We can leave aside the reduction by half of the average print run of works in the humanities, the concentration of sales on a few lead titles, and those book fairs where, besides the current year's Goncourt prize (though not last year's), only the stands reserved for the authors of comic books, the memoirs of a star or the indiscretions of a peak-time television presenter have lengthy waiting lines. No book of 300 pages, duly annotated, will replace in the forum the live commentaries of the good customer. The length or breadth of obituaries speak for themselves: no picture, no homage. Words no longer leave a trace, letters neither, and 'only traces make us dream'. Thirty seconds for Julien Gracq or Michel Tournier on the evening news, twenty minutes for Prince or David Bowie. The great cleavage is no longer between bosses and workers, but between those who have a face and those who do not. The visible and the invisible. Hence the success of Facebook: finally, a face for everyone. Narcissus is participatory. Marx analysed the relations of production. When will we have an analysis of the social relations of representation?

The fibs of an injured yuppie? Admittedly. But the domination of the read by the seen has not just transformed our lectures into viewing sessions. PowerPoint is obligatory. Many new professions can only welcome this change in delivery: plastic surgeons above all, but also designers, graphic artists, decorators, headline writers, layout artists, lighting engineers, stylists, window dressers, retouchers, hairdressers, packagers, and so on, and what scribes, typographers, proofreaders, binders and booksellers have lost, in terms of scale and importance, gives employment to others. Besides, literary culture has done enough harm – think of the tragicomic *Little Red Book* – and great readers chopped off a lot of heads over the last few centuries. A well-behaved chap like Julien Sorel would not have lost his head on the guillotine if a copy of Napoleon's *Mémorial de Sainte-Hélène* had not fallen into his hands, and Mme Bovary would not have taken arsenic if serial novels had not turned her head. Visual culture has brought us pretty faces – many young Iranian women used to have their noses changed for that of Vivien Leigh in *Gone With the Wind* – but also deaths and torturers: the decapitators in Iraq and Syria are youths intoxicated by Hollywood trash films. Every preferred medium has its train of victims. To return to the main point – if the new facilities of exchange have opened the play of images to every human being able to tap on a keypad, and the crazier you are the more you laugh and cry, you will note, without too much chagrin, that the pleasures of all-visual have as their counterpart a reality not augmented but diminished. It is enough to take account of what does not find a place on the (recorded) image, to note the realms of the personality that can atrophy as the result of a hypertrophied optic nerve.

An image is positive: absence, project, the possible, the programme, everything that goes beyond, anticipates or questions the actual given, is in no way photogenic and cannot even be photographed. WYSIWYG: *What you see is what you get*. We must therefore always be positive, forgetting the old work of the negative. Farewell dialectic and contradiction, and welcome submission to that which is, respect for the fait accompli.

There is no image of the universal, the impersonal, the ideal or the abstract. Still less in close-up. You cannot photograph France, capital, justice or the bourgeoisie. All that is truly real is the individual, the particular. Farewell the common and the collective. Farewell the general will. Welcome, *tout-à-l'ego*[5] and your own coverage.

You cannot photograph a relationship of subordination or consecution, a hypothesis or an inference, a proof or an induction. Farewell to concern for coherence and logical rigour; objective truth counts less than authenticity of expression; hello to blag and bluff. Shock video and fake news are synonyms.

You cannot photograph 'For a long time I went to bed early', or 'Rise up quickly, desired storms', or 'It often happened to me that I . . .' Into the trash with the durative, the optative, and the frequentative. Bye-bye to the sense of duration and the taste for perspectives. Hello, the fixation on the immediate; now everything is now.

Our visual field has grown, our symbolic field has shrunk. There are certainly several kinds of intelligence. But that which André Malraux once defined (a strongly European one, at that) – 'Intelligence is the destruction of play-acting, plus judgement and the hypothetical spirit' – must be pronounced obsolete. By inverting the terms, we obtain a working definition of the intelligence in command today: the construction of imposture, plus the absence of distance and the impossibility of hypothesis.

Sic transit the objective mind!

Happiness above all

When was it first seen as natural to smile at the camera lens? 'Say "cheese" . . .' Since the end of the Second World War, at the call of Time Life, whose stars then set the tone for the profession of photography. Look closely at family albums,

---

5 A pun on the phrase *'tout-à-l'égout'*, meaning connection to mains drainage.

magazines or portraits from the time when the little bird still popped up. The serious look serious, the joyful have eyes that sparkle, the tired have a tired demeanour, the old are old, and the ugly are ugly. The rictus is not compulsory. You are what you are. 'Keep smiling' was not yet the law. The order to smile, extended to the smiley on our screens, allows only a radiant wrinkle. Frowning is ill advised, and a dark look a serious mistake. We are sometimes asked by the photographer to jump in the air – always movement. Enthusiastic, optimistic, young. Never old, never unhappy. *Happy birthday, happy hour, Happy New Year, happy ending* ... A leitmotiv. The idea that Saint-Just declared in the course of the Revolution to be 'new in Europe' had already been engraved by Thomas Jefferson in the American Declaration of Independence of 1776 as an inalienable and self-evident right: life, liberty and the pursuit of happiness. But the two ideas of happiness were not the same. The one had Locke and Epicurus behind it, the other Aristotle and Rousseau. The first meant a promise of well-being given to each individual, the second meant the extension to the plebeians ('the unfortunate are the powers of the earth' – Saint-Just) of the means to live with dignity. A private happiness founded on the cult of the crucified is paradoxical. America is a 'theo-democracy' (Jean-François Colosimo), the child of the *Mayflower* Puritans and William Penn's Quakers, later imposing on itself Prohibition, the Hays Code and the most meticulous sexual repressions, only to give birth to *Playboy*, striptease, and the adoration of the Golden Calf in the name of Moses. All recreations that we do not immediately associate with the strait-laced Calvinists of Geneva. Free enterprise as the key to beatitude makes individuals entrepreneurs of their salvation, but the form that the Reformation took in the United States changed its very content.

Let us start with good humour, so desirable. In the land where 'everything is possible and everything is the biggest', optimism is the very foundation. For many reasons, first of which is that there is space, which protects against tragedy, something that thrives in confined places, if possible without skylights. A prelapsarian geography, regenerative, without corruption or tyranny. A past that weighs little and passes quickly; happy peoples have no history (from which it follows, as Valéry wrote, that 'the suppression of history would make people happier', QED). The necessity to restore morale in the face of natural catastrophes, more cataclysmic than elsewhere, earthquake, tidal wave, fire, tornado, flood (in Europe catastrophes are more political in kind). But also, the mental tranquillity of the insular: the troubles of others do not reach me, I can carry on as if nothing had happened. An economy, today, of services and consumption, which has a greater need of the smile of the sales clerk than the production of machine tools or coal mines. Communicators have to show themselves welcoming, cordial and engaging, which is not the first concern of the transmitter or the teacher. Tocqueville, however, had already remarked, long before the age of the void:

> Not only does democracy lead every man to forget his forebears, it also hides from him his descendants and the lives of his contemporaries, leading him constantly back to himself, and threatening finally to enclose him entirely in the solitude of his own heart.

This retrenchment, subsequently known as individualism, has always been a bedrock of American Protestantism. 'My spirit is my church,' said Thomas Paine. And Thomas Jefferson: 'I am a sect unto myself.' The ego factor, characteristic of a religion that needs no institutional intermediary to address God, where it is possible to live out one's faith without the aid of a priest, encouraged – this is one of its happier effects – the sense of individual responsibility and psychological exploration. 'God being closer to me than my own intimacy'

(St Augustine), I converse with myself in speaking with God. Hence the growth in the drugstores of the me-literature and self-help shelves, pompously labelled 'wisdom', and a penchant for euphoriant psychospiritual therapeutics, Oriental and sometimes egoistic. The other side of this pragmatic faith, along with the incense stick and meditation, is known as the dollar.

The European faithful do not worship in the Son of God the first of our business leaders – 'He chose twelve men at the bottom of the ladder and made them into an organization that conquered the world' (Bruce Barton, *The Man Nobody Knows*). One that guarantees good business, and makes a large bonus a sign of belonging to the elect. Christian Europe does not separate the theology of glory from the theology of the cross, or envisage the advent of the kingdom happening without serious preliminary vexations. It even holds that discovering Good is painful. Saul became Paul by falling off his horse, and martyrdom is still the surest way to achieve sainthood. The way of the cross is extremely rare in churches across the Atlantic. Pentecostals celebrate the descent of the Holy Spirit on the apostles in Jerusalem by song and dance, and the good news relieves the bad news that preceded it. It is the Resurrection without the Passion, Easter Sunday without Good Friday, dawn without sunset. What Americans call 'positivizing'.

Tocqueville wondered, when he heard American preachers, 'whether the main object of religion is to procure eternal felicity in the other world, or well-being in this one'. We could say that the latter stands in for the former. It is impossible to imagine the 'Protestant pope' that was Billy Graham denouncing, like Pope Francis, 'the imperialism of money that is establishing a world economic dictatorship'. In the context of this plutocracy blessed by Heaven, the proletarian can vote for the billionaire, thinking that this is a candidate who no longer needs to use power to enrich himself, and that the finger of

God is already on him. And in this theo-democracy, a sui generis mixture of plutocracy and theocracy, there is no longer any limit on campaign expenditure (6 billion dollars in 2016). The thirst for profit is inscribed in a theology, since, according to Billy Graham, the fire that the Bible speaks about is not the eternal fire that burns sinners, but the inextinguishable thirst for God. Nothing is more painful and gloomy than a religion of salvation with neither Hell nor sin, a messenger without Pietà or crown of thorns. When religiosity rhymes with prosperity, when individual achievement counts as spiritual accomplishment, the gate-keepers of paradise no longer have to dress in black and beat their breasts (or anyone else's). No room for flagellants here. Neither for Dostoevsky or Kierkegaard. Everything starts again from scratch. The guarantee of a second chance has as its ideal or foretaste not baptism but anabaptism. You can be baptised at any age, and everyone is entitled to a second birth. The reborn Christian can start again on a new footing, wipe out defeat and rediscover innocence. In a group, like Alcoholics Anonymous – an association that came from America, a collective confessional where each communicates to the others, as a good and sociable sport, their recent performances in the matter of abstinence.

Sometimes hysterico-fusional, the neo-Evangelical Barnums turn their backs on monasteries and catacombs. They're great. They're visual. They're musical. It's 'marketing'. It's 'fun'. It's crazy. It's healthy. It's useful. It's lucrative. It's everything. And it works. It's made to work. Happiness redeems you from the stain of being yourself. The unhappy consciousness is not 'made in the USA', and Manichaeism is equally far removed from both Jesuit subtleties and exalting Pascalian impasses. Whereas a Europe scalded by harsh proofs has been able to reconcile itself to the tragic, in good times or bad, to 'potter around in the incurable', a history with safe conduct in which God wields the final cut protects you from the irremediable. The collapse of the Twin Towers on 11 September 2001 may well have seemed to some people a foretaste of the apocalypse, but it did not undermine the theology of hope, the attraction of which is not readily belied. The United States remains 'the land of the future' that it was already for Hegel, 'the country of dreams for all who leave the historic armoury of old Europe'. Useless to point out that revolutionary romanticism, the motive force of which is nostalgia and ultimate defeat its dark confirmation, has no place in the homeland of wonder boys and success stories. The new civilization despises losers, the poor and the defeated. It has no sense for the grandeur of lost causes.

What interested the Roman was to act; what interested the Greek was to be. To 'do the job' demands immediate responses; to care for your being lets questions ripen. The Roman trusted in his gods; the Greek suspected them, and not without reason, which led most Greeks, apart from Archimedes, to neglect tool-making, rather than spurring them to make our valley of tears more liveable, by harnessing rivers, building dams, inventing medicines, finding solutions. 'Tomorrow is another day', a performative belief, is the first message that the Statue of Liberty addresses to the immigrant reaching Ellis Island: here, your being will be what you do. To see only the good side of things has itself its good side, sufficiently mobilizing for the less good to be forgotten. This reduces the rate of human unhappiness, and helps to soothe our ills. Resilience, for example, is an American concept, and we can only rejoice at seeing it so well taken up in the Latin world by our psychotherapists, to overcome our psychic and physical traumas. Prometheus had every interest in showing optimism, to find ways of extending life expectancy, relieving pain, curing diseases that were formerly incurable, repairing violated women and abandoned children – in sum, not laying down his arms before the inexorable and fatalities. Americanism, in this sense, appears as a Prometheanism enhanced by faith in providence. It is understandable that the evangelical nebula with its multiple sects is spreading across the Americas, the West Indies, and Asia. A prodigious success: to have forged at one stroke the spirituality of the rich and the millenarianism of the poor. Protestantism revised and corrected by American civilization is flowing out to remodel the old fiefs of traditional religions.

What, according to established teaching, is the age of innocence par excellence? Childhood. Americanism, which sacralizes that age, invents for it the finest games and toys, amusement parks, the Yule Log, Mickey Mouse and Bugs Bunny. Was it not to children that the kingdom of God was promised? When are adults happiest? When they once more become children. How can they be helped in this? By filling them with ice cream, milk products and sweets. And by putting plenty of carbohydrates in their drinks and foodstuffs, at the risk of making them obese, but that is the price of painless happiness, the sweetener. Soda, burger and donut. Existence still presents some tiresome activities, school for example. But everything is done there to avoid boredom, to make the teacher into an activity organizer, the textbook a TV programme (the double page modelled on the screen), and the lesson itself a recreation. Listen to a lecture? Really boring, but a preventive starting joke. Read a heavy volume? Refer to *Reader's Digest*. Bury someone close? Entrust their body to an embalmer, who will give it back to you in the funeral room, titivated, made up and spruce. Hear about the sad state of the world? Infotainment, news as a game, or feel-good TV. The disabled are rebranded as 'persons of reduced mobility', and wars as external operations. People no longer die; they leave you or pass on. To spare us 'the trouble of thinking and the pain of living', our model has a practical sense better than genius. In kitsch, which is the technique of happiness for all, its engineering seems unbeatable. It includes the basket of candies at the hotel reception, the baby talk in our adverts, and euphemisms everywhere. Not to mention laughter workers, a constant background of music in public places, cemeteries hidden in remote suburbs, life as a right and not a gift – in sum, the organized evanescence of anything that might remind the little premature infant that, for all their efforts, at the end of the day they are vulnerable, precarious, and even, dare we say, mortal.

Sapiens europeus has so well taken to heart the lessons of 'everything's ok' that they accuse themselves of being down in the dumps each time they forget to smile at the latest novelty, and to signify urbi et orbi that the world as it is fits them like a glove. In case of objection, they will be called, and will call themselves, spoil-sports, protestors, moaners, worshippers of the past, shirkers, sulkers, archaic, misanthropic, utopian – descriptions designed to be pinned on the defeated species by the winning species. Valéry had already seen it coming, this transatlantic transfusion: 'Not knowing how to cast off our own history, we are being discharged of this by happy peoples who have no history or almost none. These are happy people who will impose their happiness on us.' The civilized (in the sense of colonized) take double doses in their duty of felicity at the best price; this is the eternal problem for those seeking to make up for lost time: taking the worst of the mainstream and leaving the more refined to the metropolis. We know nothing of the mystical background of pop sects, the divine perspectives of gospel music or the great hopes of Martin Luther King. The terms 'providence' and 'manifest destiny' make no sense in Europe, while 'optimistic' means being relaxed in the daytime, chic and sensual by night, but always arty. In Paris, the Zadig and Voltaire boutique displays in its window 'an optimistic new hit bag in natural snake or vintage green'. Consumer optimism is the shop without the chapel, or the shopping version of millenarianism.

To reach conformity with the mother house would imply, to be rigorous, putting a minus sign on a number of sentiments or states of mind that *Sapiens europeus* has up till now marked with a plus sign, having drawn from them a number of harmonious and even euphoric chords: spleen, contemplation, reverie, ennui, melancholy (the happiness of the defeated), sadness, amorous chagrin, and bunking off. Everything that helps set to music the wretchedness of people without God (or even with God, the fodder of the sectarians), and that certain returns of a carefree civilization that loved dreams, chimeras and sunsets bring back as a distant memory. 'Andromache, I am thinking of you!' 'Ariane, my sister, how wounded by love', 'I heard an ominous voice say / Well Guillaume what you are doing here'. Perhaps one should, by way of prophylaxis, ward off the ailments of happiness by circulating a collection of chosen extracts, a portable anthology titled *The Horror of Happiness*. For the French part, we would find, along with Baudelaire of course, Flaubert – 'Happiness is a monstrosity! Punished are those who seek it'; Jules Renard: 'The happy and optimistic man is an imbecile'; or Léon Bloy: 'The modern world: an Atlantis plunged in a junk-yard'; Marcel Proust: 'For happiness is healthy only for the body, it is chagrin that develops the strengths of the spirit'; Emil Cioran: 'Anyone who succeeds in everything is necessarily superficial;' and many other complaints of the same kind, hardly with the scent of saintliness. The Louvre museum, for its part, to make up for the dramatic fall in the number of American tourists in Paris, could move its El Greco, Caravaggio and Rembrandt collections down to the stacks, and replace them with *Balloon Dog* by Jeff Koons, Félix González-Torres's *Candy* installation – sweets of all colours wrapped in cellophane (to be regularly renewed) – and Nam June Paik's *TV Cello* (art video). It could simultaneously launch, by a vast campaign of spots, clips and tweets, a new political organization: the party of happiness.

The three governing axes analysed above allow us to reply, concretely and without harshness, to the eternal question: what is a successful life? Not to miss anything, necessary and sufficient on top of a good level of income (dollars, euros, yen), are: 1) to be visible (work your image, brand, identifier); 2) be in movement (shift, surprise, advance); 3) be good in your skin (fit, young, dynamic). In other words, branding + running + fitness.

From each according to their abilities, to each according to their needs.

5

Why Do We Still Close Our Eyes?

Nothing need be said about things that go without saying. America is the herald and bastion of democracy, the guarantor of international order, the protector of the free world. Radical Islam is the great and only threat to our civilization, which is ever more inclined to submission. And 'Europe, my future' will make us all stronger, more prosperous and cooperative. Not to subscribe to these three truisms amounts to excluding oneself from the orbit of reason and from local culture. This is genuinely intimidating, enough to stay well behaved. And it is well worthwhile asking why.

'We knew all that. And yet, from laziness, from cowardice, we let things take their course. We feared the opposition of the mob, the sarcasm of our friends, the ignorant mistrust of our masters'.[1] Fear still influences our judgements. French intellectuals, even those reputed to be 'free spirits' (but who claims to be otherwise?), do not cogitate on a backroom 'stove' in an unknown Amsterdam street, without newspapers, blogs, tweets, TV and radio – like our patron saint Descartes. They are subject to certain atmospheric and local pressures, which set down red lines that no one crosses without penalty. In international affairs, there are Normandy beaches on which it would be dangerous to disembark with your nose in the air and a flower in your rifle, overlooked from the cliff top by a *Blockhaus* with gun loops able to settle the matter in a few

---

1   Marc Bloch, *Strange Defeat*, p. 172.

words. Defence on this Atlantic Wall is economical, and can count on the victory of the short term over the long. In the videosphere, small is beautiful, and I am preparing to be rather long.

Anti-American, useful idiot, anti-European: so many stones that it is not good to hang round your neck if you want to get ahead. Best to follow the leader, with an evasive smile. To put dots on the i's you need character, which is not given to everyone. To unbutton yourself is indecent, still more so in the context of an investigation that claims to be even-handed, and white coats are de rigueur in a laboratory devoted to studying the comings and goings of power on planet Earth. Yet a pinch of personal history may cast a clearer light on a disconcerting chiaroscuro. Even if discredited by its deadly use in the Communist world, self-criticism is a genre still authorized in the age of liberalism, where a rather conceited one-man show even brings great success.

On 'The Star-Spangled Banner'

Contrary to my twin, Hibernatus, rescued from his carefree existence after years in the deep freeze, I did not visit EuropaCity. If it is true that you do not see the grass growing, or fading, and that intermediate seasons and interregnums are hard to fit into a chronology, it is a bit much to wait seventy years to realize that your biotope, where it is good for you to live (all things considered), has slipped from one magnetic field into another. This negligence has attenuating circumstances, the first of which is due to a personal malformation that has grown into a 'social question': a certain cowardliness of character, expressed as concern for one's reputation. The flesh is weak, and Panurge is concerned above all else to spare himself trouble. Having long since lost the battle of epithets, the out of place are no longer entitled to inspect the labels that opinion, queen of the world, sticks on their backs; and the stigma of 'anti-American' ('simplistic' can be added), halfway between fascistic reactionary and mental retard, was and remains one of the most unpleasant to wear in contemporary Paris. The fact of figuring among the usual suspects, by dint of a record that is not quite clean, is a further dissuading factor. I will not deny that certain little misadventures, while contributing to my instruction, have led me to be doubly cautious. Such as finding myself, one April day in 2001, under arrest at Boston airport, where I had arrived in response to a university invitation, with my passport confiscated, and expelled from the country after questioning. Suspected of maintaining 'contacts with terrorist organizations', I figured on the blacklist. This enforced return home – with a ban on revisiting or even overflying what these sentinels of a spotless land represented to me as a holy ark – inspired in me less resentment than gratitude, so rare are the occasions, *intra muros*, for reflecting on the elasticity of the words 'democracy' and 'terrorism'. These inflatable structures depend on who is blowing them up, where and when.

Having closely read various anthologies (and particularly *L'Ennemi américain* by the excellent Philippe Roger, which lists the more or less inept or comic expressions of anti-Americanism by French intellectuals over the last two centuries), I could not permit myself any illusion about the cohort of sorry ancestors that anyone venturing into this minefield would join. This 'stupid and mean phobia', this 'endemic animosity', this 'mental slavery', reach a peak of insanity in the case of the citizen of a country that, contrary to Germany, Italy or Spain, has never been at war with the United States, and a peak of ingratitude on the part of a spoiled child who has twice been saved from the worst by the GIs – 1917 and 1944. Informed into the bargain that 'negation is the obligatory prolegomena to any deployment of anti-American rhetoric' (Roger), it could not escape me that my unconditional admiration for Miles Davis, William Faulkner, Ava Gardner, Dashiell Hammett and Orson Wells, combined with an irrepressible sympathy for *Homo americanus* (having had the good fortune to meet several counter-examples of both sexes), made my case all the worse in the eyes of these vigilantes. I am one of those people whose love of France is equalled only by their allergy to the French as individuals. And just as the 'average French' archetype strikes me as unbearable – narrow-minded, stick-in-the-mud, uptight, afraid of risk and high winds, a kind of 'bad-tempered Italian' – so I find their transatlantic counterparts – open, direct, generous, accessible, inventive and often funny – immediately attractive.

To make a point of method here. The French, the European and the American are ideal types here, in the Weberian sense of the term: neither facsimiles nor inductions from the particular to the general, but intellectual constructions that make it possible to study collective singularities. A concept that seeks the unity in phenomena that can be photographed is not a photo. It goes without saying that an American from Boston is not the same as one from California, that Southerners see themselves as very different from Northerners, and whites from blacks, just as Danes are not Sicilians and the people of Marseille not like those of Calais. There is no possible zoom in on 'the American' or 'the European', no photo booth for the soul of a people. Our intoxication with the trace has put a blindfold over the eyes of the mind. There is the concrete, in the street, and there is the grasp of the concrete, in the head. Common sense is well aware of this when it deals with 'brand images' of nationalities in TV series and travel guides. The French bashing so popular in the United States does not take such precautions – no more than does the French kiss. We can add that archetype or prejudice often end up as an 'ego ideal': we conform to this more or less consciously. Abroad, we often play at being

French, and by playing we become so (which is rarely in our favour). The French may be doubtful of their archetype, but their particular features leave foreigners in no doubt, particularly Anglo-Saxons who observe, read or visit us: arrogant, pretentious, believing themselves more intelligent than they are, and dirty into the bargain. The refined version: fine speaker, not without charm. The low version: big-mouthed and two-faced, with a talent for treason (see films and series). French lover or double agent. Charles Boyer or Marcel Dalio. The names of actors change; the roles remain. Those who do not like stereotypes lack practical sense. Business textbooks in *globish* know more about us than we do ourselves.

To continue.

'It is well to distrust first impulses', said Talleyrand. Incapable of switching in a single moment between Gobseck[2] and Rockefeller, or rather between Martine Carol and Barbarella, I have always trusted Talleyrand's judgement, and am not far from applying to the champions of America, for my personal actions and the order of my sentiments, the formula of one of our old revolutionaries, Stanislas de Clermont-Tonnerre on his Jewish compatriots: 'For them as individuals, everything; for them as a nation, nothing.' The best, therefore, is to avoid detection. If I defined myself as an 'anti-imperialist', which seems infinitely more exact, I might well be accused of intending to mislead. The devil can be recognized by his art of mimicking the angels; that is the basic rule of every inquisitor mastering his trade. In short, 'anti-Americanism' is a game you are bound to lose: by denying it you admit it, and by confessing it you only get what you deserve. A bad deal.

The blacklist has more than one box, and not ticking any of them makes the charge all the more serious. I could not

---

2 Jean-Esther van Gobseck, principal character in Balzac's novella *Gobseck*, representing a typical usurer of his epoch.

espouse the classic complaints of M. Perrichon against his benefactor.³ The country seat against the skyscraper? As a commoner, I rate elevators still better than steel and glass. The 'Belgian America' of Baudelaire, boring and hating beauty? My ancestors were Belgian, I am proud to say, and I do not hold the beautiful made-to-order known as art, which appeared only in the fifteenth century, an indispensable hallmark of civilization. 'High culture' against rather barbarian trinkets. 'We call barbaric', wrote Montaigne, 'everything that is not our custom.' The mind against the mechanized society? Denouncing the dangers of the machine and progress in the name of the bucolic sweetness of the countryside, the inhuman metropolis in the name of the country town, preferring yokels to merchants, the woollen stocking to the bank account – this Pétainist bleating, the hallmark of pre-war anti-Americanism – could only raise a smile in a mediologist, conscious that there is no mind without machine, no civility without city. The post-war personalist version – the old saw of 'humanism against technology' – was no less acceptable for a disciple of the ancient historian André Leroi-Gourhan, who taught us, beyond possible argument, that hominization went together with technicization, cortex with silex, that the tool is not the opposite of the living being but its extension, and that *Homo faber* and *Homo sapiens* are one and the same species. Catholic against Protestant? The repugnance of a Mounier or a Claudel,⁴ who wondered whether the two vertical bars of the dollar sign were not the horns and tail of the devil, continued a religious quarrel that does not concern me. The enemies of supposedly reformed religion, champions of an obsolete and historically lost cause, resistance to the Yankee, are not

---

3 *Le Voyage de M. Perrichon*, a comedy by Eugène Labiche and Édouard Martin, recently made into a film.

4 Emmanuel Mounier, founder of *Esprit*, and Paul Claudel, writer and diplomat, both associated with a spiritualistic Catholic revival.

cousins of mine. In short, an ideal case for investigators able to unmask false pretences.

On top of the handicaps of my character ('character is destiny'), I perceive today two more common blinkers that explain, without excusing them, my inadvertences.

First of all, blindness by ecosystem. A goldfish should not be asked to organize a conference on fishbowls through the ages. Had it a sense of history, it would not see any interest in this. You do not discuss the notions that you discuss with. To expect a man in a bath to describe his tub is the same as expecting the giant Baron von Münchhausen to rise from the ground by pulling himself up by the hair. Successes of this kind are rare. The business of 'bringing this troublemaker into line' has been going on since I was in short trousers, but I was one of very many who missed the pseudomorphosis that was under way. That is the term used when one mineral replaces another while keeping the form of the latter. Or, if you prefer, when a great country remains a member of the Security Council, with embassies, an army, a flag, ministries, prefectures, and so on, while the inside of the shell has been hollowed out and given a different filling. Our framework of thought and action, being precisely what enables us to think and act, is bound to escape us. Any consciousness of it means taking a distance, a suspension of membership that cannot be expected of a sponge living the life of a sponge. You have to remove yourself from your milieu to obtain an exact view of it. Brazil was a lookout of this kind for Stefan Zweig, where he died in 1942 (at Petrópolis, after completing *The World of Yesterday*), as likewise for Bernanos, a fellow exile who never recovered. Casting off the moorings always means taking a risk – and remaining in one's bubble is a biological precaution.

As a result, there is a habit left over from the Christian drama: overvaluation of the event (happy or unhappy). This congenital superstition makes us insensitive to the silent transformations dear to Chinese civilization, better armed intellectually than we are to grasp flows that work unperceived.

'Europe has dramatized the event, as with the Book of Genesis, or the break, as with Christ, but also by way of newspapers and the novel; yet any event is like a figure that hides us from the background out of which it arises. The event is a line of foam dancing on the depths' (François Julien). A slow impregnation does not make the front page. The paradox is that we constantly celebrate change or call for it, whereas our dependence on the event (and its corollary, the obsessing face of the leader or head of state) prevents us from becoming aware of it. The flashes of nonstop news veil from us as many profound continuities – 'The Republic, our kingdom of France' (Charles Péguy) – as solvents of continuity. The failure to prioritize among news items, combined with the intensive bombardment of brains, teaches us much about how the world is going, but nothing about where it is coming from and where it is heading, and the current degrading of the event (inscribed in a series, which recapitulates the old and announces the new) into a media coup (bare-breasted FEMEN suddenly appearing in a cathedral) does not settle anything. The more informed we are about what is happening, the less we grasp what is coming and what is disappearing, whether it is the subjunctive tense and the ham sandwich, flânerie and the briar pipe, or the prime time jingle (*chanson de texte*) and the upturned thumb replacing Churchill's V-sign; and conversely, what makes a noise or a clash leads us to forget the steady lengthening of stock-market reports on the radio, like weather bulletins, the appearance of a 'money supplement' in the evening paper and the periodic return of the Dalai Lama on the front cover of magazines, alternating with backache and the secrets of the Freemasons. To take up Julien Gracq's image, still astonished by the *Jeu des mille francs*[5] that he hears every day, and by the

---

5 A long-standing general knowledge quiz game on the France Inter radio station, still popularly referred to by this original name though since 2001 it is officially called *Jeu des 1,000 euros*.

participants' knowledge in every domain: in the year 2000 we have more points on the map than in 1900, but far greater difficulty than our forebears in tracing the contours that link some with others. We know many things, but they do not make sense. We have more information and less perspective.

It is this comfortable dodging that makes possible such vile neologisms as *cosmopolitisation, globalisation, transnationalisation*, all kinds of *ions* that have fallen from the sky, ominous and unquestionable; and, distracted by this ceaseless riot of details, to push back the moment for pruning a hundred insignificant trifles, such as the 'Happy Birthday to You' on the cake, the hand on the heart of the footballer when hearing the 'Marseillaise', followed in due course by the minister and finally the president, the 'Mr' Dupont on the envelope instead of 'M.' (for 'Monsieur'), the 'New York City Police Department' T-shirt of our head of state jogging in Manhattan, the dropping of the preposition '*de*' (the 'Brive Festival' or a 'rebel attitude'), the first name as acronym (VGE, PPDA, BHL),[6] 'human rights' instead of the rights of man and the citizen, the 'desk' for the reception, 'low cost' countries and the *Figaro's* 'talk', *Art Press* fronting the newsstands, or a thousand little foreign inventions of which *sourçage* [= 'sourcing'] seems trivial. I put some down to naivety, and blame others on Sarkozy, a spoiled brat from Neuilly who became president while still adolescent, and others again on a fashion with no future. Not to mention the most serious thing, Anglo-Saxon common law, more favourable to business, prevailing almost everywhere over Roman civil law.

I was wrong in attributing these faux pas to a solely political slippage, a 'slide to the right' from the centre of gravity. An old house tradition. Have not the imperial powers always had their fifth column in the kingdom of France? Under Henri IV,

---

[6] Respectively, Valérie Giscard d'Estaing, Patrick Poivre d'Arvor, Bernard-Henri Lévy.

the Spanish party was the Catholic League; later, the English party that of the house of Orléans, our immortal *juste milieu*; the Soviet Union had the Communist Party, and its disappearance shifted our El Dorado from east to west. Unstoppable. Uncle Sam filled the empty box of paradise on earth, and found champions among the neo-Orléanistes back in business, the 'republic of the centre' heralding 'marriage for all' – the right of the left with the left of the right. Not enough difference to go crazy for. Anodyne alternations that will never make a dent in the crystal of France, an indestructible figure that will live so long as there are mouths to vibrate the silent '*e*' of alexandrines on the dais, and fingers for the circumflex accent in dictation. In short, geological and pedagogical alibis were available to avoid the painful balance-sheet. When I saw, the day after 11 September 2001, the front page of our evening breviary headlined 'We are all Americans' (rather than 'New Yorkers'), I immediately interpreted this as a cry from the heart, a praiseworthy reflex of identification with the victims, or even an explicable slip on the part of an editor freshly moulded, like nine out of ten of his fellows, by the French-American Foundation, which invites all reputed young leaders to meet twice a year, for an extended stay, the authorities and stars on the other side of the Atlantic. A high-level kneading for our higher officials, I thought. The plebeian body of the nation would not surrender. Everything suggested that my fear of proclaiming myself would be echoed by a fear of jumping to conclusions, and of seeing as partisan excess an impartial fact, that of a simple act of civilization applicable to all, Greeks and Trojans, rendering really puerile the ancient divisions into Armagnacs and Bourguignons, left and right, progressives and conservatives. The ecosystem takes in everything, without bothering about detail. And so, for a long time, I went to bed early, closing my eyes to the ceaseless transition of things.

On the fertile crescent

Good republicans can always give a good cause a bad prognosis – in this case the intransigent defence of secularism. Especially when they are too sensitive to the spirit of the time, and a legitimate reflex of self-defence ends up taking the place of reflection. Let us remember briefly the familiar words on the street and in the press, which every terrorist attack in one of our cities cruelly confirms as self-evident: 'The democratic West is at war against an enemy that wishes its death. The Islamization of our societies of Christian origin is under way. The pressure comes from many sides: aggression and subversion, terror and demography. That is the real threat, to be combatted in every way, including by law. Not to decree a general mobilization would amount to surrender.'

This has been repeated by governments, the audio-visual media and the newspapers ever since the collapse of the Twin Towers in Manhattan, an image that made the world tremble like no other before it. The bloodshed that has followed in its wake, in many corners of the world, has only given credence to this cast-iron sentiment, midway between anger and panic.

It is useless to go over the recent epidemic of radical Islamism (an eruption foreseen and explained by Arnold Toynbee back in 1947), which has made a hundred times more victims in the Islamic world than in our own, and has been very well analysed by excellent scholars. Nor to examine measures of prevention and repression, as has been done by eminent jurists and specialists in public security. What needs to be questioned is the way in which an immediate danger, certified by pools of blood on the pavement, has been able to grow in our minds to the point of becoming the sole sword of Damocles posing a mortal threat to our civilization.

Without making an ideal son-in-law, the terrorist is the child of our so-called postmodern societies – illegitimate, but natural. Terrorists apply to the letter the established laws of operation. *Economics* first: minimal investment in terms of personnel, material, logistics and money; maximal profitability, in terms of corpses, but also and above all in noise and fury, which are the pursued objectives. The *minimax* of the weak – a murderous avatar of 'less is more' – turns the defences of the strong, who are forced to the opposite formula: maximum investment, and very limited results. Then, *information*. How is this defined? By the inverse of a probable occurrence ('the bishop who bites his dog'). What gives it greatest performance? Miracle and massacre – the two masterpieces of the unexpected in time of peace. As a machine to produce the event, productions conceived to ring out, astonish and shatter people, terrorist action in the age of technical reproducibility possesses an unprecedented viral capacity, since it is immediately duplicated in millions of photos, instantly brought to our home or our pocket. With a lorry, a gas bottle and a Kalashnikov, a crazed individual, whether acting alone or under control, but anxious to get to Paradise, can spread fear among tens or hundreds of millions of people. The cheapest panic, with, for the desperado, a guaranteed magnifying effect on the target side. A shift in our collective unconscious, continuous but unnoticed, of a molecular kind, without shock or fracas, amounts to an anti-event, the soft swaddling of every day; bloodshed in the open air, a super-event that strikes the heart, but awakens instead of putting to sleep. The explosive jihad, which thrives on misfortune, incites people to a spiritual counter-jihad, designed to tense the relaxed springs of a collective personality. What better service than to restore a 'we' to a formless aggregate of disunited 'me's'? Toynbee saw every civilization as a response to a major challenge – a thesis broadly confirmed by history. A few hundred French jihadists in Syria, plus a handful of poorly organized kamikazes in Europe, hardly stand comparison with the Golden Horde or the Viking longships. But this supposed cataclysm that one year caused 150 deaths in France, this sporadic mini-guerrilla amplified by the videosphere, may have something of the challenge that the British historian deemed indispensable, for both the inception and the strengthening of a civilization. In the words of Xenophon, 'It is the act of a wise man to draw profit from his enemies.' An enemy is a strengthener.

Habemus papam! White smoke, relief. *Habemus diabolum!* We retch, we restart, we repair. What? An erosion. A civilization always needs barbarians, and when it lacks these it invents them. Our civilization did not need to invent this enemy. It was there, revulsive and therefore galvanizing. Nothing is more depressing, for an alliance or a coalition, than a former enemy who abandons his role and gets chummy, and we might recall the sardonic warning of a Russian diplomat to his American counterpart at the time of the dissolution of the Soviet empire: 'You're being punished, we're depriving you of an enemy.' Also worth remembering is the haste of the Atlantic alliance in the years that followed to avoid breaking up after this disagreeable evasion, by immediately finding, at the cost of a great state lie, an honourable substitute – a distant dictator who was dressed up as an Islamist for the needs of the cause (not to mention the blind alley to which this frenzied quest committed it).

The jihadist is the ideal barbarian, almost theatrical with his long beard, his bare feet, his black tunic, his cutlass and his Kalashnikov – ideal because controllable and absorbable over time. In the short term, this unpleasantness is deemed more important than the collateral damage caused to the rule of law by the 'war on terror' – emergency laws, extrajudicial executions, colossal expenditures, systematic surveillance of allied and suspect populations, and so on. Not counting the perspective of a war without the possibility of either decisive victory or concluding peace treaty.

It remains that a sacrificial ideology with a minority vocation does not make up for an organic weakness in terms of real power, and we will hardly see an American president follow the example of Constantine and suddenly convert to the straight path of the Koran. No one can accept the presence of individuals who wish and do us harm (to whom, in fact, we ourselves return eye for eye and tooth for tooth, but far away and without cameras). But giving our Enlightenment back the outside darkness that makes it stand out better, like antimatter to matter, or black to white, is not a benefit to disdain. A warrior, macho culture, atonal and self-centred, raises the value of a pacific, musical, feminist and future-centred civilization. Everything for the group, vis-à-vis everything for the individual. What contrast could be more opportune for each side?

Real and dangerous enough in the Maghreb, in sub-Saharan Africa, the Near and Middle East, likewise in the Caucasus and Indonesia, this pious fury also has extra-religious motives in Europe, bound up with the state of the world: the explosion of migration flows, drought and climate disturbance, the need for labour in the industrialized countries, the ageing of our populations, the galloping urbanization of the planet (400 cities of more than 1 million inhabitants in 2016, against 16 in 1900), identity inflammations of all kinds (multicultural coexistence is very rarely ecumenical), the failure of secular Arabism (to which the West contributed). To all of which can be added, in our own country, the collapse of the educational system, mass unemployment, the rifts in the social fabric, a collective imaginary dried up by the supremacy of economics, the crumbling of secular messianisms and the workers' movement, the rebound effect of colonization ('You came to my country without asking me, I'll do the same'), the scant interest we pay to the culture of immigrants, and so on. That said, apart from certain towns in the Midi where a pious Maghrebin can feel at home, there are countless cases in France of integration, mixed marriage and successful social insertion. And certain reputed demographers see this convulsion as an upset characteristic of 'holistic' and traditionalist societies when they leap with bound feet into individualistic modernity, which should in time be pacified by a combination of mass literacy and birth control. Whatever the prognosis, there are a certain number of facts that should reassure the guardians of the parish steeple and the paranoid of the minaret: the clash within Islam between Sunni and Shiite, the lack of a major country playing a leading role, which neither Egypt, Turkey nor Iran can claim, for obvious reasons (even if Pakistan has the bomb, and Arabia the oil), the national fragmentation of the umma, the non-existence of a solidly established headquarters like the Comintern, and the fact that the Muslims of France are the least community-minded of all communities present on our territory. The Koranic puritanism that is exported, a culture of the decultured, a refuge for the deterritorialized, certainly has the privilege of still smelling of sand and camel, the quarrel around the well and the women in the tent, but it cannot compete with our multicoloured and catch-all syncretism.

The jihad certainly has its enthusiasts and its preachers, building castles in the air and starting with Europe. Bolshevism in its day had the same, and did not hide its desire to sell the last capitalist the rope to hang himself as soon as possible. Its doctrinaires, with their threatening writings, sowed considerable fear in both prefectures and families. Utopia rebounds from age to age, from secular faith to religious. The question is to know whether these megalomaniacs have the means to achieve their ends, and in the present case there is good reason to doubt this. A security threat does not amount to a *civilizational offer*, something that Islam is unable to propose. It can cause disorder, but not constitute an alternative order; damage civility here and there, but not tear a civilization to pieces. Besides which, no empire is forming today in this region of the world (without empire, no civilization), but on the contrary a steady dismantling of established states; and you would look in vain for the cyclotron, industrial patents, sex appeal, scientific discovery, films, engineers, an original economic model, an element of domestic comfort, an unusual beauty – in short, a new arrangement of life. The rejection of accommodation with the world below can lead to secession – of the monastic or fanatic type, ascetics or Hashashin, but this will only ever be an ersatz, not a replacement solution for the long term. Which is not to deny the fascination that the mystique of a body-and-soul commitment may exercise on adolescents who are offered nothing substantial in their own country. Nor the time bomb that the constitution of counter-societies full of resentment can represent for republican cohesion if nothing is done to tackle the problem (and particularly a measured control on immigration). An alternative project requires other means than intimidation, or even, at the worst, the occupation of a few interstices. As for the 'great replacement' of the French population that is heralded by some talented fear-mongers, this is quite perplexing. Apart from the fact that France is the only European country with a fertility rate of two children per woman (due in part to this recent immigration), it is hard to see how some 60 million people with full stomachs, the American dream in their heads and consumption in their hearts, could be subjugated by half a million of the most deprived who go to the mosque on a Friday, out of the few million 'Muslims' for whom Ramadan is as much a social ritual as a religious one (the notion of Muslim being extremely vague). Apart from a few town centres where café owners refuse to serve women, with satellite dishes on the balcony and prayer rooms in the basement, the capture of minds and imaginations seems limited to a few pockets without great influence. Do our economists speak of a 'Mecca consensus' that might challenge the 'Washington consensus'? How many Islamic companies are there among the major global suppliers of Internet access? Do the children of our ruling class want to pursue their higher education in Riyadh, Baghdad or Tehran? Or are our advertising agencies, our multinationals and our banks moving their headquarters to North Africa, the Middle East or Indonesia? Do the European Union, the Fondation Saint-Simon, the World Bank in Washington or Sciences Po in Paris propose to replace English by Arabic in their lectures and communiqués? In France, the number of teachers of this language (the second most spoken in our country, and one of the ten working languages of the UN) is dwindling from year to year, and the CAPES[7] in Arabic are held only every other year, for lack of candidates. This shows a certain lack of concern on the part of our leaders great and small, since it is always necessary to learn the language of your enemy (as the young officer de Gaulle learned German).

Is there any common denominator of the Western nations other than GAFA (Google, Apple, Facebook and Amazon)? I do not rule out having my head in the sand, but I cannot see the language of the Koran being adopted tomorrow, nor a 'Muslim transversal' acquiring the scope and impact of a substitute globalism. The 'Western camp' calls itself the 'international community' – as people speak of international art, fusion food and world music, meaning 'made in USA'. There is no 'Islamic camp', and if, per impossibile, the fifty-seven countries of the Organisation of Islamic Cooperation, whose seat is in Jeddah, should one day manage to create one, it would never be able to present itself as the embodiment or vanguard of humanity in general. The Arabic and Muslim world remains *a* world: rich as it is in cultural memories and human resources, it can only nibble at our own, not subvert it, lacking the power to globalize. Its only universal, in practice, is capital, which contains nothing to scare us: it is our own creation.

Islam is therefore a preoccupation, but not a threat. We can close the authority of clandestine Islamic schools. But not pretend we are preparing for combat with an invader. When

---

7 *Certificat d'aptitude au professorat de l'enseignement du second degré*, a teaching qualification.

our Europe imagines itself a citadel under siege, with its walls shaking, we might wonder if it is not blinding itself to how it is in the process of making Europeans out of other peoples even in their own countries.

A blue flag with twelve golden stars

This great hope initially had everything going for it. St Thomas Aquinas and Victor Hugo, a happy mixture of Christian inspiration and humanitarian anticipation, generosity and likelihood. The inexorable advance towards unification of nations in a global governance, as formerly of regions into nation states, or again such strong and simplistic certainties as 'union is strength'. To which I would add, for my own part, the shadow cast by the European Paul Valéry. Undoubtedly the 'possible Europe' for which he called was not the same as the European Union. It was not a resurgence harking back to the Holy Roman Empire, but the Europe of Albert Camus and *la pensée de midi*:[8] sunny and Mediterranean, with a Catholic veneer, later becoming humanist, although closer to Rome than to Frankfurt. It began in Algiers, passed via Alexandria to Beirut, stopped off in Athens, put out a shoot towards Istanbul and then climbed north, up the Italian boot and the Iberian peninsula. And it attached the same strategic role to language, geometry and the creations of the imagination as we attach today to the Dow Jones index and the rate of corporation tax.

To give flesh to this old hearth of civilization, Valéry looked for a 'politics of the mind', which he sought to conduct in the framework of the League of Nations. This idea, initially American (President Woodrow Wilson's

---

8   The title of an essay by Jacques Chabot on the work of Albert Camus.

fourteen points) but not ratified by the US Senate, became a concrete expression of the European spirit based in Geneva – as today's UN, established in New York, is a product of the post-war American mind. This first system of collective security, lacking an armed force, failed the test when it had to move from fine sentiments to practical operations (the UN likewise, but it will have lasted longer). The most suitable leading body of this institution, in his eyes, should be the International Commission on Intellectual Cooperation, which established its offices in Paris in 1922. Valéry soon invited Einstein there, the friend and correspondent he had met in Berlin in 1926 – a closeness that brought him the nickname of 'Franco-German *rapprocheur*', lambasted by Maurras's Action Française. Our pilgrim of peace wanted 'the men of the universe' to serve as mentors for the League of Nations, so that the workers of the mind, men of letters and science who set aside personal interests and passions, could inspire the politicians in charge.

To focus his action on 'élite opinion' was perhaps not very democratic, but it was based on the hope, like a two-stage election, that 'action exerted on those who think might influence those who govern'. And that is the project that the author of *Charmes*, as travelling salesman for what is really important, went off to promote for two decades in Zurich, Prague, Vienna, Oxford, Lisbon, Rome and Berlin. This initiative from above would make our Brussels commissioners smile with pity, not to speak of our broadcasting heads, managers and lobbyists for beetroot, steel or pharmaceuticals. The new-look European became pragmatic and matter of fact. That is its whole problem, which it sees as a solution. Beneath the aura attaching to the nineteenth-century European dream, that of banquets, it has constructed the Europe of the twenty-first century, one of bankers, the most inconsistent of all dreams. How? By espousing the utopias of *Homo economicus*, the generic name for transatlantic man.

Universal history has always had more than one ruse in its bag. And so it entrusted the expansion of the American principle to what was supposed to be its counterpart and, for some people, its competitor: the United States of Europe. Such is the miracle of hegemony, to have its agenda fulfilled by someone else. It is also that of love. The young America knew how to make itself loved in the aftermath of the war, something that its then rival, the Soviet Union, could not have done. And whoever loves, imitates. It is not abnormal, therefore, that the federal Europe of the future should have attempted to build itself by extending to the Old Continent the dogmas and manners of the New. To work with such application to efface its personality, to enthusiastically unravel everything that made up its DNA, is a theme to interest a playwright, who might hesitate as to the register to follow, comic or tragic, Labiche or Sophocles, given that there is material to laugh at here as well as to cry over. The EU is an antipolitical machine, which certain people dream should become a political actor, even expecting it to establish itself one day as a power, when its raison d'être is precisely to flee any idea of power.

To resume the story. Social Democrats and Christian Democrats, the two leading actors in the play, had in the aftermath of the war, to prevent any future flare-up, the excellent project of making the common interest prevail over the particular. Against the sin of nationalism, federal redemption. OK, why not? After which we saw the socialists of the day dismantle social protections, deconstruct the state, the last and only possession of those who have no possessions, to purge public services and enthrone the supreme law of profit, while those in charge of the intellectual side set up an entity without heart or soul, the most crudely materialist of human aggregations, where the lobby is king, the calculator is queen, and the refugee an enemy. The best pupils in the European class thus extended to the Old World the culture of the New. What is abusively called 'Europe' probably did not trigger anything; it accelerated the movement of what is called globalization to the point of completing this. How? By working *on the economy*, in the conviction that a political federation would follow, with no problem of continuity, the production of coal and steel. And that a geographical expression would become a source of historical energy simply by assuring the circulation of people, goods and capital in the context of 'free and fair competition'. Bypassing, therefore, the vicissitudes known to all strategic players in the arena of powers. The shortcut turned out to be a blind alley. And so the European Union did not escape from history, as has wrongly been said, for the reason that it never entered it.

No army had ever developed under the flag with its crown of stars taken from the words of the Apocalypse, nor has a Brussels herald vetoed anything, called a peace conference, started or stopped a war. It is not the house style. Rather, it is by agreements between governments, by a classic and judicious co-operation between sovereign states, that the great European successes, Airbus and Arianespace, were born, which have done more for the cause than an institutional artefact whose contribution will have been to franchise the globalization of a financial capitalism foreign to both Rhineland and Colbertist models. Not without launching, meanwhile, the excellent Erasmus programme of university exchange, which deserves a salute despite its modesty: thirty-three contributing countries, but just 1.3 per cent of the Community budget; 3,000 scholarships per year, principally for business and engineering; and 3 per cent of French students, including 1 per cent of university students who leave to study elsewhere. The Middle Ages did better in terms of mobility, but the effort is worthwhile.

All that remains of what is still on paper the world's leading industrial and commercial power, past master in the art of transforming its potential strengths into weakness, are two ingredients which in combination are supposed to make a giant: a great market framed by a large number of procedures. What subsists of a community of acquisitions owes very little to local culture: it is the formula 'economics + legalism' that presided over the growth of the United States of America, but from which the key third element is missing – God, the mandate of providence, the eye in the triangle, the unifying transcendent.

There was a bad situation right at the start, given that a French-American businessman, the banker Jean Monnet, sought from a concern for effectiveness to apply the methods of his adopted country, forgetting what had enabled this to coagulate, its biblical-patriotic religion. Violence had twice been the midwife of the United States – the War of Independence and the Civil War – but this assistance would allow us to avoid the habitual pains of childbirth that no federation or confederation, from the Swiss onwards, has so far been able to escape. Europe would be the exception that confirms the rule: a federation without federator, an immaculate birth, a victory with no battle. Stalin gave flesh to this hope, as the necessary opponent, but once the socialist camp collapsed, the pragmatism of small steps deteriorated into auto-suggestion, and eventually into a prayer wheel. This continues to turn, gradually slowing, but the heart is no longer in it, the officiants are deserting. It is not their fault. The chanters end up going to sleep, and the Europist cult is the first secular religion that has been unable to offer its followers an identity card, except in the form of Monopoly money. And to console them for the lack of an impossible common narrative, the bank offered them a common currency, with the idea at the back of its mind of a boundary to be pushed ever further forward. The extensive as substitute for the intensive, further on instead of ever better – *Go east, young man* – is a formula that works in a continent that has a minimum diversity in a maximum of space, but not in our own, where you have maximum diversity in minimum space.

To destroy a sentiment of belonging without putting another in its place is always dangerous. The risk is tribal retraction, a false remedy and a true poison. Political religions – and Europism was one, in its manner both oblique and pallid – evaporate quite quickly if sap is lacking, and particularly for lack of a guardian, a vertical. The Europe myth faded all the more quickly for having assumed that a constitution could find anchorage without a shared language, memory or legend. This dry and insubstantial patriotism gave way to the unimpeded spirit of commerce, holding what gives this meaning, the commerce of minds, to be negligible. Nothing is more shattering in this respect than the failure of the project for a European digital library, proposed by Jean-Noël Jeanneney when he was president of the Bibliothèque Nationale.

What is European about our aligned Europe, covered with a blue mantle of supermarkets, successor to the 'white mantle' of churches, with here and there, by way of spiritual supplement, accessible museums where cultural obligations can be fulfilled with a yawn? There was more Europe in the age of monasteries, when the Irish St Columba sowed abbeys on four corners of the continent. More at the Battle of Lepanto, when Savoyards, Genoese, Romans, Venetians and Spaniards fought the fleet of the Grand Turk, under the auspices of Don Juan of Austria. More in the peaceful Age of Enlightenment, when Voltaire played cards with Frederick the Great at Sans-Souci, or when Diderot stood at Catherine II's shoulder in St Petersburg. More in the age of Louis Aragon's *Les Voyageurs de l'impériale*, or when Clara Zetkin stirred the hearts of French workers and Jean Jaurès rallied German socialist congresses. There was five times as much Russian and German taught in our schools in 1950 as there is today; there was more Italy then in France, and more France in Italy, than there is now. We follow from day to day the vagaries of American domestic politics, and Hillary Clinton's coughing fit during her presidential campaign was the opening item on our TV news, but we have just ten seconds for a change of government in Romania or the Czech Republic. Satellite broadcasts and our intellectual laziness put New York on our doorstep, Warsaw in the steppes, and Moscow in Kamchatka. The excellent Franco-German TV channel ARTE hosts no regular debates between thinkers or artists from the two banks of the Rhine, though between the wars, when the Kiel bridge was closed, their predecessors formed an ongoing discussion club. The only daily newspaper that connected our respective élites was American, the *International Herald Tribune*, and its editorial offices have now left Paris for other skies. The last go-between for Europeans has fled to Asia.

The guiding idea of Europe, and its raison d'être, was always to oppose any ambition of universal monarchy. It drew its strength from its rivalries, and oddly enough, the concert of its nations gave it its tone. Its language was always translation, yet now it is monolingual. Donald Tusk, president of the EU, who addresses his various interlocutors in *globish*, seems far less European than emperor Charles V, who spoke Spanish to God, Italian to women, French to men and German to his horse. Of the thirty-odd centralized agencies of the EU, twenty-one offer their websites exclusively in English, and the recent Italian labour law is called the Jobs Act. To see Brussels officials communicate in a language which is that of the IMF and World Bank, but since Brexit only of one of its smallest members, is rather ridiculous. Those who deplore that this chatterbox Carthage is becoming a vast Switzerland should rather present this confederation as an example: there people regularly speak three or even four major languages, as every European should.

Strength of desire, strength of hope. We do not desire something because it is good; we deem it good because we desire it. And we had the best reasons in the world to desire a Europe federated and even integrated, in the aftermath of a cataclysmic civil war. Yet we have succumbed to a project that envisaged integrating Turkey, on the grounds of its being a NATO member, but not Russia – as if Dostoevsky, Prokofiev and Kandinsky were not more European than the whirling dervishes, as if our Europe owed more to the Sublime Porte than to St Petersburg. Only a mad economist, and a derivative one at that, could impose on a centuries-old patchwork – in which, rather unusually, the common was not always the similar – elementary geometries midway between pastiche and trophy. 'Man is a bad conductor of reality', said the poet Pierre Reverdy, and self-protecting illusions have the merit of staving off the painful moment when you discover that the emperor is naked and the truth is sad – and that yesterday's 'queen of the world' returns as a humble follower in the world of today. It is not the least of our misfortunes that the life of collective hopes is increasingly short, while our own life expectancy is increasingly long. This lack of synchrony obliges us to witness, in our own lifetimes, the ruin of the credo of our youth, whereas in the age of revealed religions, disillusion took several generations, and it was possible to negotiate disappointment, as the early Christians did, year in year out, with the advent of the kingdom expected the day after tomorrow, but postponed from one century to the next.

Certainly no one could have foreseen, at the start of this failed odyssey, that central and eastern Europe, what Milan Kundera called 'kidnapped Europe', would become after its liberation a little America to the east, where sex shops, McDonald's and heavy metal would rapidly replace bookshops, taverns and symphony orchestras, where the Pentagon would install its advisers and the CIA its secret prisons. Nor that the fertile tension between Latinity and Germanity, between Galileo and Kepler, which has given our peninsula such richness and was still alive in the Europe of the original six, would resolve, with the enlargement to twenty-eight, to the benefit of a Germany that has meanwhile become, for the sake of expiation and redemption, the most Americanized of

European societies (primacy of the economy, urbanism, federal organization, government by judges, and so on). It was so as not to hurt Uncle Sam, the guardian on whom its security depended, that the Bundestag, by rejecting the Elysée treaty, torpedoed the project of a 'European Europe' presented by de Gaulle in 1963, one that would assume the mantle of a major and independent entity. If it is true that every bird story ends with a cat, it was not said that a salutary defence reflex in the face of a political despotism would turn thirty years later into a kind of economic despotism – albeit easier to tolerate – as if no to Joseph Stalin meant yes to Milton Friedman. This was not written in the stars. The wartime generation, the inmates of Buchenwald and Dachau, the fighters of France Libre, the survivors of the Resistance, who had put all their faith in this fine project, had no reason to envisage such a collapse.

The idea that an institutional mechanism can give birth to a people in flesh and blood has therefore had its day. What remains is an undertaking without driving passion (whereas 'nothing great is done without passion' – Hegel), a Potemkin clock to be rewound from month to month, where the force of habit makes people take seriously things that are not serious. European defence is a swindle, which everything indicates will remain so, given the 'horror of battle that haunts peoples grown old' (Élie Faure); European diplomacy remains, for want of any armed force, a declaratory pantomime for internal use, with no visible effect on any theatre of operations. The foreign affairs department writes music for an orchestra without instruments. As for the European Parliament, which does not represent a people and has no initiative to make laws, it is a parody (in France, a deputy for Pas-de-Calais does not represent their constituency, but the French people as a whole). That people with good motives can wax eloquent about these indecent displays, continually elaborate rescue plans and repair programmes, offers a further testimony of the hold that all these comforting illusions still have over us. Let us only pray that a Europe that dreams itself post-tragic does not turn out, post festum, to be pre-tragic – in a boomerang effect of a striking supranational phraseology and a host of raging little nationalisms.

One would have wished for more panache on the part of the protagonists. Wanting to taste the 'peace dividend' without accepting the least warlike effort (economic, cultural, legal, military), and imploring its guardian please to maintain its protectorate, amounts to a certain lack of dignity. It is not amoral that the godfather in Washington should be reluctant to pick up the tab for this collective resignation. Certain people hope – hope is life – that the boss's reticence will finally lead the client to behave as an adult and take their own fate in hand. For the moment, the Brussels revolving door where we see a president of the European Council disappear one moment to return the next as an employee of Lehman Brothers, another commissioner as administrator for a company registered in the Bahamas, or as expert in tax optimization, is a spectacle that should cause no great surprise: the overt fusion of the business world with that of politics, lobbies and commissions is part of the model. There is certainly nothing here to inspire respect, and as Chateaubriand said, 'There are times when it is necessary to be sparing with one's contempt, given the great number of those requiring it'. We should pay no attention. A Stoic does not have contempt for anyone.

That said, it is quite possible that one day the 'European Union' might appear to our successors as the second phase of self-destruction of Europe, after the war of 1939–45. The first attacked the body, the second is attacking the mind (in each case, an operation that by cruel irony saw itself as a rescue). Valéry, with his eagle eye, respected chronological order. Craziness first, then softening up.

The strategist Thomas Barnett, who taught at the Naval War College before working at the Pentagon, recently called on the United States not to be disheartened on account of a lost war in Iraq, and to continue to successfully project across the whole world its DNA, 'modern globalization's source code', in other words its economic model, which replicates itself automatically by 'domino effect' from one middle class to another. Japan, India, China, South Korea, and tomorrow Africa (where US troops are already deployed in forty-nine out of fifty countries on the continent). In his view, while America may no longer rule the world, the world must become America. As far as the Old World is concerned, our strategist may rest assured, and Simone Weil smile from her tomb: Barnett has hit the spot in terms of its moral and mental structures.

6

What Is New about the New Rome?

> *Empires fall one after another, and, contrary to the popular saying, they resemble one another in many features. But the American imprint has renewed the ancestral hegemonic tradition with technological pre-emption. Upstream mastery of norms and forms makes it possible to add to a system of economic capture a system of social and cultural imprints, to the point of being able to substitute the latter for the former. This is an original feature of Americanization, and also what makes it hard to escape.*

Empire

Marx's *Eighteenth Brumaire of Louis Bonaparte* (published in New York, 1852) has burdened us with a formula that is too often quoted: 'Hegel remarks somewhere that all the great events and characters of world history occur, so to speak, twice. He forgot to add: the first time as tragedy, the second as farce.' Marx was mistaken; we can now do better. Napoleon III parodied his uncle, but Lenin was not a replica of Blanqui, nor Soviet communism a farcical version of the Paris Commune. Likewise, the American imperium is not a counterfeit Rome, but a Rome squared.

It is not wrong to pin a stereotype on this great country by evoking a filiation that it claimed and proclaimed at its moment of birth. Being a republic, unique in a world of monarchies, and a slave republic at that, the comparison was self-evident. A Capitol was built in its capital, it endowed itself with a Senate, took the bald eagle for its great seal, printed a phrase from Virgil (*'Novus ordo seclorum'*) on each dollar bill, and adopted for its motto '*E pluribus unum*' – 'let the many become one'. It would be wrong to see this ascendancy as no more than rhetoric. 'Our pure, virtuous, public-spirited, federative republic will last for ever, govern the globe, and introduce the perfection of man', wrote John Adams to Thomas Jefferson in 1813. (For ever, perhaps not. If we take the customary division between High and Low Empire, from Augustus to the Antonines, then from Diocletian to Augustulus, the first Roman Empire lasted four centuries. Its emulator, if we count from 1918, is just starting its second century. Still not very long, but a good start for a *remake*.) The choice of Athens, the owl rather than the eagle, would have lacked ambition and pertinence. The terrible Delian League set up by Athens in the fifth century BCE lasted scarcely a few decades, and the Peloponnese was a pocket theatre. For a nation that combines five supremacies – technological, financial, juridical, military and cultural – the only worthy precedent is clearly the Roman, given that the ecumene today is the planet, if not the solar system. The Athenian valued independence. He mistrusted foreigners, kept the metics on the margin and failed to integrate the vanquished. Rome did integrate, the United States too, hence their unequalled success. American patriotism, like the Roman, is capable of a wide embrace. It is not exclusive.

Let us make, as amateurs, a few atmospheric notes. Starting with the empire unwilling to speak its name. The term does not apply in the strict sense to the United States, which no longer annexes territories or occupies countries for the duration: the invasion of Texas (where the slavery that Mexico had abolished was immediately re-established), the taking of Hawaii, Guam and the Philippines, the occupation of Cuba and Puerto Rico, all belong to the past. 'Imperial republic' is more exact; the Roman superpower likewise maintained its republican scenery and titles in its first few centuries. Caesar and Augustus declined the title of emperor, except in the sense of commander-in-chief of the armies, and it was not until Trajan that the purple cloak was donned. Napoleon I also muddied the distinction. 'The government of the Republic is entrusted to an emperor', in the droll words of the senatus consultum of 1804.

'Grandeur and decadence' is a tag used by every self-respecting moralist. But between Montesquieu and ourselves there has been what was formerly known as an 'epistemological obstacle'. In the words of Malraux, who disliked the mechanical and always preferred legend to history (with happy results): 'The United States is the first nation that has become first in the world without having sought this place.' First of all, the count is wrong: it is the second, after Rome. Then, every imperium relies on a differential of power, not an official programme. It is not a project, but a mechanism, a forward flight by way of emergency response to unforeseen challenges, which force an advance so as not to retreat. A possible attack is prevented by another; the freedom of the seas has to be safeguarded, supply lines secured, trade outlets obtained, recalcitrants punished. The emporium, the economic stranglehold, precedes the imperium, political domination, and the two are interwoven. A war gives a boost to production (and puts an end to unemployment), and a surplus of products at home requires trade counters abroad. To defend our markets, the naval strategist Alfred Mahan maintained in 1890, we need a powerful navy, and therefore strategic bases here and there, and so also a body of marine soldiers. No overall plan, rationally conceived and methodically applied. It was only Charlie Chaplin in *The Great Dictator* who played with a papier mâché globe. The 'thousand-year Reich' lasted only twelve, the Napoleonic Empire little more. The will of a megalomaniac turns out to be sterile. If there were lessons from history, the first of these would be that good sentiments are more rewarding than bad, and that the first duty of a predator is to be a good Samaritan, in its own eyes as well as those of others. Why seek to excuse a normal exercise of power, in other words one normally exorbitant, given that no one else does so? We hardly need a lawyer to argue: 'My client did not behave very well, but it is not his fault; he did not intend to do ill.' What era has not had its hegemon, its ruling and directing nation? And what leading country, whether democratic or not, has not had its war crimes, its torturers and its hecatombs? Sumeria? Babylon? Pharaonic Egypt? The France of Louis XIV? The Germany of Wilhelm II? The England of Queen Victoria? The 'pros' who ignore the misdeeds of their champion deserve the same ironic smile as the 'antis' who demonize by ignoring the benefits. Lawyers and judges do an honourable work (though unequally rewarded), but those who confine themselves to listing the series of dominations should leave the Salvation Army. There is no prize for virtue to be awarded. It is not the fault of Rome that all barbarians, or almost all, wanted to become Romans, any more than that of the United States that so many others wanted to become Americans one day. This clogs the pipes, but no wall has ever stopped the flows of hope and hunger. *Hope dies last.*

However we might decry the orgy of analogies, it is hard not to get drawn in. We should note first of all the importance of language, which was the common foundation of medieval élites – above the national idioms derived from Latin – as English is today the common foundation of global élites, the cult of law as instrument of pre-eminence, the omnipresent religiosity. Rome was the land of the *fides*, of faith in a supernatural mission engraved by Virgil on the shield of Aeneas. 'Our form of government has no sense', said President Eisenhower, 'unless it is founded in a deeply felt religious faith, and I don't care what it is' (his own faith was Presbyterian). The mission of the United States, to ensure the happiness of humanity, was entrusted to it by God. That of Rome, by Jupiter. 'I've fixed no limits or duration to their possessions: / I've given them empire without end' (Virgil, *Aeneid*, book 1, 275). Or again: 'Roman, it is for you to rule the nations with your power, / (that will be your skill) to crown peace with law, / to spare the conquered, and subdue the proud' (Book 6, 850). The manifest destiny of the United States also spilled over its frontiers. Lincoln, in 1862: 'the last best hope of earth'. Wilson, in 1917: 'American principles . . . are the principles of mankind and must prevail.' Hence the tug between vocations simultaneously contrary and complementary, exceptionalism and universalism. To remain on its island, well apart from others, *America first*, but also to share its excellence and its values. The bipolar alternation, systole/diastole, phases of messianic intervention (generally the responsibility of the Democratic donkey) and phases of isolationist withdrawal (reserved more for the Republican elephant). There is the empiricism and pragmatism of domains of excellence: town planning, architecture, engineering. Lifting machines, aqueducts, amphitheatres, animal harnesses (though not the stirrup, a key invention of the barbarians), hypocaust (central heating). The energizing is preferred to the speculative, practice to philosophy, the robust to the delicate. The formidable military machine, capable of cleansing and integrating the foreigners; the homage paid to the veterans; *vae victis*, woe to the vanquished and the losers. In all such cases, the city is clearly a sponge absorbing peoples, beliefs and talents from every direction, today Hispanic and Asian, yesterday Africans and Illyrians. In both cases we see family dynasties, whether father and son, such as Vespasian and Titus, Marcus Aurelius and Commodus, George Bush and George W., or brothers such as Domitian and Titus, John and Robert Kennedy. A quarter of a century with two patrician families at the helm. And, of course, panem et circences, bread and games. As far as bread is concerned, the first Rome, with its *annona*, wheat for all, showed itself more socially responsive than the second.

Then there are the political leaders.

Kissinger addressing a student seminar: 'When you first meet Reagan and you spend half an hour with him, you leave saying: "Oh my God, how could the future of the free world be dependent on such a stupid guy?" ' Then he added: 'And yet every move he makes is right.'[1] Destiny is accomplished through the unpolished as well as graduates. Charlemagne never learned to write, but his reign relaunched the study of letters in Europe. Election campaigns in Texas would cause candidates to blush in a by-election in the Creuse, and the personalities of those elected, given their responsibilities, sometimes leaves us gaping. Those who are astonished to see boors and showmen established in the White House should turn to their textbook on Roman history. Augustus, Hadrian and Marcus Aurelius were the exceptions, just like the Roosevelts, Kennedy and Obama. Commodus was a bodybuilding histrionic, Heliogabalus went about his tasks dressed as a woman. Instead of peanut farmers or reality TV stars, it was dancers, coachmen and hairdressers who wore the imperial purple. Caracalla was mad, but it was a good idea to extend Roman citizenship to all free men in the empire (212). And why should the captain, who only sits on his arse, escape the threesome that governs us all – lust, cupidity and vanity? The follies of the Capitol never prevented the empire from attaining its war aims.

Polite exchanges between conqueror and conquered go in each direction. The educated Greek saw the Roman as a rough-hewn boor, a big child easy to trick, a brave soldier, a good administrator, vulgar and badly spoken. Conversely, the *graeculus* was seen as an unreliable wimp, brilliant but

---

[1] According to Tom Wolfe, 'Tom Wolfe's View of Trump', *American Spectator*, 30 March 2016.

cowardly, just as the figure of the Frenchie is either the little marquis or the surrender monkey. Either the select, the language of fashionable people (as Greek once was), or the hair-splitter. Marcus Aurelius wrote his diary in the language of Plato, and Stoicism, Greek theory, Epictetus and Menander were debated under the porticos with the same fervour as French theory, Derrida and Foucault today. The sons of the rich, the *gens togata*, made their Grand Tour through Attica, with its schools and museums, just as their successors, guidebook in hand, come and look for their prehistory in Florence, Westminster or Versailles. That said, the potentate fears the effeminate, and the Roman senators were ordered to address their Greek interlocutors only in Latin. This would not prevent the empire, however, in its mature years, from cultivating a high-flying syncretism, of which Marguerite Youcenar gives us a taste in her *Memoirs of Hadrian* – an astonishing mixture of refinement and brutality. The first term in the White House seems today in escheat, and we no longer know whether former presidents write their memoirs in French, German or Spanish.

Let us dig a bit deeper. God has the reputation of writing straight with curved lines. America traces its curves with straight lines. Like the Roman, it has 'square feet'. It loves the right angle, its towns are rectangular, its roads straight and its soul either black or white. It demands well-drawn boundaries, moral or physical walls. The binary suits it, and not the nuance, the labyrinth or the chiaroscuro, specific to the European as well as the Greek. This is the sense of *fines*, the clarity of demarcations, that was so cruelly lacking in the Greek archipelago, as in the ectoplasm of Europe today. It is in the idea of the boundary – spatial, temporal, grammatical and political – in the need for clear and clean definition, that Umberto Eco has very rightly located the organizing core of the Latin archetype. The legendary foundation of Rome was made by the tracing of an inviolable boundary line (Romulus and Remus), and its deconstruction, a thousand years later, by the gradual effacement of the *limes*. Eco writes:

> If the time ever comes when there is no longer a clear definition of boundaries, and the barbarians (nomads who have abandoned their original territory and who move about on any territory as if it were their own, ready to abandon that too) succeed in imposing their nomadic view, then Rome will be finished and the capital of the empire can just as well be somewhere else.

The so-called European Union, whose citizens are still seeking their Ariadne's thread and their contours, seems to suffer from similar uncertainties.

What is most striking, in this diptych, is the embracing machine, the melting pot that was so lacking in Greece, as the Roman historian Tacitus well observed. 'What other cause was there for the ruin of the Lacedemonians and the Athenians, despite their warlike valour, except their insistence on dismissing the conquered as foreigners?' (*Annals*, XI, 24). The Romans could give their successors a lesson on this point. A president of the United States has to have been born on American soil, but a Roman emperor could be born in Gaul, Spain or Syria. And the right to sit in the Senate was extended to the Aedui, a Gallic tribe, in the first century CE. What a national culture dare not do, an imperial civilization allows: the hyphenated citizen. The Gallo-Roman, the Chinese-American, the Italo-American. A win-win solution. The double attachment. Literary circles welcomed foreign authors such as Seneca, Lucian, Quintilian or Martial, and this generosity was well repaid. The finest declarations of love and allegiance to Romanity were those of Spaniards, Berbers, Jews and Gauls (and our best publicists, in France today, stand comparison with Polybius or Flavius Josephus). By respecting local civic contexts, whether Hellenic or Celtic, the patrician dynasties were able to ally with exotic aristocracies and convert client into kin. The empire of the West does the same, albeit to a lesser degree, and, just as in those days you enriched your great homeland with the small one of your native soil, it is current in the global élite today to couple their small homeland, their nation, with a greater one, the American. This double membership has become customary in Europe as elsewhere, and two passports are a commonplace in Boulogne-Billancourt or Neuilly. The latest arrivals in the 'Western family' are habitually the most loyalist. In southern Gaul, the Aedui, won completely for the metropolis, solemnly condemned as anti-Roman those Gauls who championed their nation's independence (in accents that sound familiar to us today).

What a dignitary of a Celtic or Gallic tribe lost in terms of sovereignty, wearing the toga amply made up for in increasing his opportunities for contact with high spheres, offering all kinds of honorific position, decorations and juicy outlets. Without forcing his talents, he was bound to thank the Empire for having brought peace, as well as roads, a postal service, and better hygiene (stadiums, spas, and running water). How can we not understand the sadness of Rutilius Namatianus, the Gallo-Roman of the fourth century who had established his dwelling in the world-city, but was forced to return to his native heath after the sack of Rome in 410?

> We sing of you and always will, while fate allows –
> Every man alive remembers you!
> Accursed oblivion will hide the sun before
> The honour that I owe you leaves my heart,
>
> For you extend your gifts just as the sun his rays
> Where all-embracing Ocean ebbs and flow,
> The Sun, who holds all things in place, revolves for you:
> His steeds both rise and set in your domain,

For you were not slowed down by Libya's flaming sands;
the Bear, though armed with ice, has not stopped you.
As far as your life force has stretched towards either pole,
So far your courage spreads across the lands.

From many different peoples you have made one nation:
Even bad men profit from your rule.
Because you offer equal justice to the conquered
You have made one city of the world [...]

Wars justly fought and peace, not domineering, brought
Your noble glory to the height of wealth.

What you rule is less than you deserve to rule
And you surpass great deeds with your own.[2]

Who knows whether the sublime ruins of Manhattan, a few centuries from now – not before the end of the millennium, we may hope – will not inspire in a long naturalized Eurorican an ode of gratitude equally lyrical and convincing?

In such conditions, what makes for the American 'extra'? First of all, a more favourable geographical situation, the ideal longitude: midway and mediating between the two oceans, the balancing arm between Atlantic and Pacific, a more propitious position for mastery of the seas than that of Great Britain. Our central island, a land reserved and preserved for the Good, is physically better protected from foreign invasions than was the *Caput mundi* (a death blow from the air remaining a striking exception). Here there is no Brennus, no Gallic hordes creeping up in the dark to awaken the geese of the Capitol, nor a Hannibal stamping the sacred soil with his elephants. It is possible to strike without being struck. To send an armed drone 6,000 kilometres from Arkansas and return

---

2 Translation Martha Malamud.

home for lunch with your children. Finally, and above all, this American 'extra' is based in inculcated procedures that, in the present case, have no need for submission through weapons. Rome's habit was to extend *manu militari* onto foreign lands near and far, to colonize territories with its peasant-soldiers, before imposing its customs. *Carthago delenda est.* After which Carthage was destroyed stone by stone, the Punic territory annexed as a province with colonists from Italy – veterans or undesirables – and reurbanized after the Roman model: aqueduct, baths, amphitheatre, altars. For our own 'indispensable nation', military occupation is in no way a sine qua non. Naturally the sheriff has a Colt, and President Theodore Roosevelt carried the big stick indispensable for talking softly but wishing to be heard. This can go as far as the nuclear and chemical devastation of enemy territories ('Agent Orange' in Laos and Cambodia, where more bombs were secretly dropped in a year than on Japan and Germany during the whole of the Second World War).

But the military is only an extra. After victory, Vietnam was Americanized, in a way that Germania was not Romanized. Absorption has made progress. The underlying contract, since time immemorial, remains the exchange of submission for protection; blackmail is part of the deal, and sanctions if need be. But more often the protectorate is solicited, even implored, as in the case of Western Europe after the war. This was in its own interest, for both production and defence. Resources were lacking for essential reconstruction. A good and true empire is an empire by invitation, where the client tugs the boss by the sleeve. What else are Central Europe and the Balkans doing? The Baltic states, Georgia and western Ukraine? The tutelage of a distant power is always better tolerated than that of the immediate neighbour – Russia in this case.

What is piquant is the traditional contrast between the desire to govern the planet and the lack of curiosity towards those who inhabit it. Between the global perspective and the provincial mentality of a giant sufficiently confident in its lucky star to feel dispensed from paying any real attention to the outside world. Just as its *leadership* can only accept a cosmetic *partnership*, so theological confidence makes concern for ethnology superfluous. The world leader can if need be confuse Bolivia and Colombia, even Italy and Germany, or Sunni and Shia; go and devastate Indochina, Iraq or Afghanistan, as a France and England brought into line did in Libya, without paying the slightest attention to the past, the language and customs of these countries. A senator can boast to his electors that he does not possess a passport. The metropolis accepts all diasporas, but does not delegate any prerogative. Its troops must always remain under national command – whereas the Ottoman Empire entrusted its defence to Albanians, and the Byzantine Empire to Armenians. In case of a coalition, the best 'allies' of the sovereign are better informed, but not consulted, and the auxiliary forces in Afghanistan, the French in particular, only learn in the papers the negotiations underway with the enemy or the dates of the planned withdrawal.

'The greatest danger for Rome', wrote the historian André Piganiol, 'came from its very triumph.' Danger arises from a race between clients for the award of good pupil or the title of stakeholder. Emulation overloads the boat. And the barbarian's imitative aspiration to make himself Roman made for a Rome disquiet and watchful of the challenge of overextension. In 33 BCE, King Bocchus of Mauretania bequeathed his realm to the Roman people and embraced Octavian Augustus, who proceeded to hand it to Juba II, king of Numidia, in the year 25. To make someone obliged to you a border guard makes more sense than sending a garrison out there. Fifteen hundred GIs in Uzbekistan, detachments in Poland and Estonia, an outpost in Kyrgyzstan, a gigantic base in Kosovo and others in Okinawa and the Philippines evoke the traditional danger facing all empires: succumbing to overreach. The neoconservatives have no worries over this, convinced that their civilization is a gift that no one can refuse, that the Pax Americana can only be greeted with gratitude by its beneficiaries. Tacitus had fewer illusions as to the value of Rome's values. The experience of his father-in-law Agricola, placed at the head of the province of Brittania, enabled him to divine what was at issue. 'What these men, in their simplicity, called civilization [*humanitas*], was the beginning of their servitude' (*Life of Julius Agricola*, XXI). Or again, in the words of a Scottish rebel: 'They sow desolation and call it peace.'

Among the umpteen explanations of the 'final fall', reaching from the uncontrollable surge of the Huns to the lead piping in Roman houses, not to mention the undermining work of the Christian fifth column, a bad compromise with the Visigoths and a senseless proliferation of holidays in the metropolis, one is more convincing than all others: hot baths. The softening of the hardship of living weakens the fibres, and, as Shakespeare put it, prosperity and peace lead to cowardice. Or as Ibn Khaldun (1332–1406) warned, the ex-nomad turned sedentary, more gallant than warrior, becomes feminized in his palace. The softie agrees to administer, but no longer wants to make war, and still less get himself killed. He entrusts this disagreeable mission to private armies, mercenaries or security companies. Demobilization and demilitarization, the end of military service, the taste for pleasures and the sweet far niente. The dirty jobs are outsourced to foreign legions, and the barbarians posted at the frontier to defend the empire become hard to manage, then greedy, and surge back to the heartland.

In the short term, the centre trusts in its ultra-sophisticated technological equipment to put an end to the 'troubles' on the *limes*. Referring to the outbursts of the Numidians, Batavians and then Vandals, Marcel Bénabou, a leading historian of Romanization, makes the following remark: 'The comparative warlike skills of the barbarians and the civilized gave the advantage to the former, who had greater powers of endurance. The Romans prevailed through discipline and heavy equipment.' The Romans prevailed for a time, but this did not prevent Roman Africa from 'de-Romanizing' as early as the fifth century, well before the advent of Islam. The stealth bomber, the cyber-attack, night goggles and the robot as lifeline. Up to a certain point, at least.

Given that 'all empires perish', there is never a happy end in these superproductions.

The impress

Exceptionalism is commonplace enough, often backed up by divine election, but the new empire of the West shows greater originality.

The contemporary French would not be what they are, moderately civilized, were it not that the Romans, Franks and Saxons in turn taught their ancestors how to live, manufacture, eat and calculate better. Language itself reminds us of our debts of honour. The Italians of the quattrocento helped us emerge from the Middle Ages, the English of the Enlightenment to emerge from absolutism. We can thank such people as François I, Du Bellay, Montesquieu and Voltaire, scintillating liaison agents and accelerators of civilization. Without these two countries as beacons, we would have been seriously behind in the arts of politics, painting, architecture and others. Today's hegemony may be bringing us just as notable advances, but it is of a different nature and scope. Neither the Italians of the Renaissance, nor the English with their House of Commons, nor Leonardo da Vinci, nor Locke, transformed our table manners and our habit of building castles in the air. What is exceptional about Americanization, a colonization without colonists, is its envelopment from top and bottom. From Harvard and Hollywood, Orson Welles and the blockbuster, Philip Glass and Beyoncé, Cape Canaveral and Disneyland, Rawls in the lecture hall and rap in the courtyard, Faulkner and Facebook. Through the bad boy and the hipster, Clichy-Montfermeil and the Marais, the hoodie and the dress code for the Opéra. The ploughman from Chambord did not speak a word of Italian, and did not listen to Monteverdi morning and evening. The admirer of habeas corpus did not measure his garden in inches or wear a Scottish kilt. Our promoters of the welfare state, in the Belle Époque, whose eyes were on Bismarck's Germany, did not swoon at the parades of spiked helmets or gorge themselves on Frankfurt sausages.

Our Janus faces both forward and back. One foot in the nineteenth century of nation states, when 'the glory of the individual was drawn from his voluntary participation in the whole' (Jules Michelet), and the other in the twenty-first, when the glory of the whole derives from the degrees of freedom it leaves each member. This Janus holds both ends of the chain: hyper-sovereignty – no law, nor international treaty, no Geneva Convention can tie my hands – and hyper-individualism, each able to do, say and write what they like. The United States is a land of both order and dissidence. Mainstream and underground. Male power and gay pride. Obesity and obsessive dieting. Conformist culture and counter-culture. The suburban rail line and the line of coke, the dream of the down-and-out and the model of the switched-on: Wall Street and Occupy Wall Street, the IMF and ACT UP, the devastating B-52 and the protests of Woodstock, *Robocop* and the sit-in, for Trump and against him.

In Latin America and Middle Eastern theocracies, the metropolis arms and supports dictators while at the same time encouraging the censored and the imprisoned – often in the same countries. The US ambassador in Paris calls the permanent secretary of the Quai d'Orsay in the morning to remind him that there are things one does not do as a good and loyal ally, and in the afternoon holds a discussion with the young Arabs of '9-3'[3] to encourage them to be proud of the culture, while his employees listen in on conversations at the Élysée (200 metres away) from the embassy roof. He hosts at his receptions 'everyone who counts in Paris' and sponsors a 'decolonial summer camp' (April 2016), a training seminar in political anti-racism inspired by feminist and post-colonial studies at US universities. Ever ready to lend a hand both to the helots and the lords of the earth. No other country has this capacity of operating simultaneously in the salon and the office. Its finest achievement is basically this: the existence of an ultra-patriotic society – which flies its flags at airport counters, along the roads, at the entrance to buildings, on the door of the local store, even on the lapel of the president's jacket – while its followers and champions describe as 'nationalist' the least display of patriotism in their own country, and are not far from seeing an enemy of the human race in anyone who dares to evoke national interest. What is praiseworthy for the world leader is sickening in the ranks.

We should guard against having an 'American-style' view of Americanization, in black and white. Either the United States was created by God, and anyone opposed to it is kin to the devil – the neoconservative emphasis; or alternatively, the empire being the figure of the devil, anyone opposed to it is on the side of Good – the opposite exaggeration. The wind from America has often been a wind of freedom, whether in the France of Louis XVI or, at least towards the end, in Mandela's South Africa and for many colonized peoples under European rule. The Kurds today benefit from this the most. Nor should we forget that Americanization has been and remains

---

3 *'Neuf-trois'* is the code for the Seine-Saint-Denis department, also incorporated in the name of an album (*93 Party*) by the rap group Suprême NTM.

synonymous with emancipation for women, minorities, gays; liberation of manners, freedom of expression, sexual equality. Looking at only half of the programme, the thesis of a happy Americanization is no less sustainable than its opposite. We should not forget that this other country, that of Upton Sinclair and Ernest Hemingway, Martin Luther King and Malcolm X, Woody Guthrie and Joan Baez, Noam Chomsky and Oliver Stone, is itself perhaps the first victim of 'Americanization'. Europeans must defend the cause as best they can. There are two Americas, and this is the chance for the Americanized abroad. They feel less alone, as do those at home, and each can take the other by the hand.

The extraterritoriality of American law innovates technologically by using the dollar and the Internet as means of attachment to the metropolis, but makes no exorbitant demands in terms of traditions. The Romans also placed their legal punctiliousness in the service of political expansionism. The United States can sanction rival economic actors, foreign banks and businesses, for not respecting the decisions of the Senate, and it naturally does this in the name of morality, the struggle against international corruption. You need not even have a branch in the United States to be liable to pay their fines ($8.9 billion for BNP Paribas, $772 million for Alstom, and so on), as the very fact of trading with 'enemy states' under American embargo, or transacting with them in dollars – hard to do otherwise for a multinational – is enough to make you guilty. Supported by the capacity for planetary interception and espionage (the NSA), used for purposes of blackmail, extortion and penal repression that may extend to the imprisonment of foreign heads of companies, this practice allows one of the most lucrative opportunities of 'leading from behind' (helping to finance the Department of Justice and the hundreds of thousands of lawyers of the domestic legal machine). The surprising thing is that this is seen as legitimate by its victims, who pay cash on the nail. No reciprocal measure envisaged. *Business as usual.* Systematic spying and listening in on 'allies', the obligation to hand over personal data on air travellers, the refusal to subscribe to the International Criminal Court while threatening to put the squeeze on signatory states, and ten other measures shamefacedly referred to as unilateral, are scarcely even commented on any more.

Observing the little princes of his time 'enchanted and charmed by the name of the One alone', La Boétie spoke of 'voluntary servitude'. The cowardice or personal mediocrity of our counterparts today is not in itself sufficient explanation. Contemporary sociologists have other names to describe this docility. They speak of the transition from domination to hegemony, internalized domination, desired and experienced by the dominated as a promotion. The turning point, sometimes visible to the naked eye, is when the hand on the shoulder or a similar token of condescension ('Welcome!', 'Lovely!') to the client is perceived by the latter as a promotion. When what was recently annoying becomes flattering. For de Gaulle, to have French forces in peacetime under foreign, so-called 'integrated' command, was an injury to his self-esteem. For Messieurs Sarkozy and Hollande, it is a reason for pride.

Well ahead of any weakness of minds or characters, this is above all a question of the force of circumstances. Our obeisance was not to Fort Knox, US aircraft carriers or its thousands of armed drones. What won us was the washing machine, the Internet, GPS, surfing and the music mix. More widely, everything that makes life less hard, and was either invented or industrialized – or both – in the United States a decade or two before us. From the paperback (1939), the model of our *livre de poche*, to the container (1956), the motor of globalization, by way of the milk shake and the juke-box. The empire can hardly be criticized (still less by singles and housewives) for such basic aids to survival as the refrigerator, the toaster, the vacuum cleaner, the microwave, the waffle iron, the Xbox, and a thousand other marvels. The vital is viral – full stop. Especially when the instinct for self-preservation combines with the pleasure principle – and with morality into the bargain. If we survey all that has made the human condition more tolerable and that began in North America, we are easily convinced that it would have been highly disagreeable not to follow closely behind: the tractor, the telephone, the supermarket, but also, besides domestic comfort: universal male suffrage,[4] votes for women, blue jeans, youth, jazz, gay pride, and so on. On the day of the Last Judgement, these benefits will amply balance the scales against the electric chair, 'pedagogism' and Bush Junior.

We still find it hard in France to understand that what people have in their heads is not unrelated to what they have in their hands, whether rosary or smartphone, and also on their feet, in their ears, or on their heads – boots, headset or cap. A *'caillera'*[5] can buy Nike sneakers while swearing to 'fuck' America; the one does not prevent the other, and purchases have more effects than expletives. It is life that counts, not thoughts. If our metropolis forms part of our everyday life, this is because it gives (or rather sells) us each day the means to do more with less. More products with less material, more sensations with less attention, more income with less expenditure, more kilometres with less petrol, more knowledge with less study ... And this is the meaning of our species' material progress, ever since the invention of the worked flint and numbers: more with less, which makes our laziness, physical or mental, every day more productive. In this sense, the succession of objects of genius, this ever better for ever less dear, fits readily into the direct line of evolution. And the love-hate that the land of high tech arouses among

---

4 'Universal' only for white men.
5 'Street kid', derived from *'racaille'* (scum) by *verlan* inversion, and adopted as a badge of honour.

the less favoured has much to do with the toxic/tonic ambivalence of any new machine, the worst and the best of things (whether the wheel, the alphabet, the harness or the steam engine). The same with GMOs, another American invention. There is a case both for and against. Designed to improve the yields and profitability of soya and maize, patented seeds have to be purchased each year from Monsanto by farmers who then need – a dialectical reversal – deadly pesticides to remedy the remedy. The fact remains that, constantly chasing the latest brilliant invention, each of us feels beholden to make our annual pilgrimage to the Mecca of technical norms.

Need we recall that it is our relationship not to ideas but to our material conditions of existence that determines the course of things and ideas? That the French Revolution was not the result of a Masonic plot or a conspiracy of free-thinkers? And that the modernization of mentalities was not the effect of the remarkable work of enlightened minds who sought to reconcile France with its time (Jean-Jacques Servan-Schreiber, Jacques Revel, François Furet)? We should not give in to the political illusion, a venial sin of our landscape, and even if it is annoying, mutatis mutandis, to note that 'the future of our country and our civilization is the stake of a struggle, in which, for the most part, we are now no more than rather humiliated spectators' (Marc Bloch), let us refrain from seeking the treacherous villain responsible. We are neither occupied nor conquered. 'Every conquered people seeks its Ganelon', wrote this great historian and witness in *Strange Defeat*. Our grandparents found this in Philippe Pétain, Maurice Gamelin and Pierre Laval, aged defeatists, underequipped troopers, spineless and paunchy bourgeois. It would be a cowardly abdication to make scapegoats of our managers, whether left or right, who keep in shape with CrossFit, our young-innovating-dynamic-connected entrepreneurs. Still less our 'cosmopolitan élites', a replete oligarchy or other conveniences. Do not confuse a revolution in tooling with a social and political counter-revolution, even if the former may help the latter. This is the time to return to Marxism again in the original sense of the word. 'Give me the windmill and I'll give you feudal society. Give me the steam-engine and I'll give you industrial capitalist society.' Give me the computer, the satellite, fibre optic and the container, and I'll give you the World Economic Forum, fine particles and Andy Warhol.

There are far fewer things that depend on us than do not, but among the former is one that would be best kept under control: snobbery. The English term 'snob' is a slang abbreviation of *sine nobilitate*, 'lacking nobility'. The sentiment of being in with the in crowd, of going up in the world, by acquiring those exclusive things that people in the spotlight possess and consume, drives each of us running to the shops. It is hard to temper this instinctive conviction, in as much as we are all incurable snobs, and have been at least since we came down from the trees at the end of the quaternary era.

Snobbery is stronger than elsewhere in the field of culture and 'trendy' milieus, and the playing field is level here. Snobbery here is necessary in order to operate, what Diderot would call an occupational *idiotia*, and for many people, it is a way of making a living. There is no trickery or smoke in the eyes about being *in* and *on*. You either are or you are not. For the auguries of chic and shock, what has not happened in the States is more or less devoid of interest. It's second-class. It's provincial. It's *French shit* (the excuse of a museum director presenting his collection to a visiting American colleague). Something to put back in the stacks. Hence the need to retrain or relook in order to overcome official disdain. An amusing example, in the plastic arts, is how in the 1970s Ernest Pignon-Ernest, by his situational collages, inaugurated something new: making the street a work of art. That was not street art, which generally consists in making the street an art gallery by exhibiting in the open. But when the label 'street art' was launched, much later, Ernest was misguidedly classified in this school and became *in*. The craziness of this desire not to remain provincial is that it unfailingly leads to a provincialization. But necessity makes the law. Just as our inventors have to market their gadgets in the USA, and the over-sixties do the same with their furniture by advertising on Airbnb, people market themselves by taking a surname or forename that sounds good – so that Marie-René Alexis Saint-Leger Leger became Saint-John Perse – or by posing outside the White House. The adverts for French cars not sold in the United States are filmed in Arizona. The label 'French theory' gave credence in France to philosophers who had previously been little heeded (something that amused Jacques Derrida, who, after giving a lecture in New York titled 'Spectres of Marx', saw himself reappear the next month, after twenty years in the shadows, on the front page of a fashionable Paris weekly). If a Cameroonian historian, a Haitian novelist, a Senegalese philosopher, a West Indian poet or a Quebec designer, generally relegated to second class, is approved by an American university, publisher or gallery, we gladly open our doors to them. (And our cousins are quite right to go where they will be recognized, rewarded and fêted, given that a greedy and grudging France refuses them all this.)

The backbenchers have joined the avant-garde, the politicians and cultural figures. A candidate in the French presidential election declared in Las Vegas that he intended to make France a 'smart nation'. And if they want to 'step on the gas', they take their examples either from Bernie Sanders or from Donald Trump. Charlemagne insisted on being crowned emperor at Rome to attest that his reign was indeed devoted to defending the faith. A French president, wanting to prove that his mandate will be devoted to the defence of modernity, has to follow his election by hurrying post-haste to the Oval Office for a photographic dubbing. Whether artist or terrorist, head of state, designer or philosopher, it is across the Atlantic that you have to make your impact – on minds, wallets, eyes or skyscrapers – where the return on investment is best. The young educated European, aspiring to success, may make his first waves in London, but the unction will only be conferred by a stay in New York, the *speculum mundi*, and if possible an MBA. This focus is merited. The world-city is that which receives the most foreigners and receives them best – and thus which exports the most and the best overseas. The least xenophobic is the most radiant; one follows from the other.

Imprints

We do not have to swear oaths to the standards of legions, still less kiss the slippered foot. We are neither suppliants nor flunkeys, but users. We learn what to think from our apparatuses. And government by norms, being far more painless and less costly than by blockades and fines, is a model of economy of forces. It is a straightening out (the meaning of '*norma*' in Latin) rather than a bringing to heel. Training and retraining is done by use alone. The pre-emptive normalization of technical systems – education, health, transport, media – produces a dynamic that does not present itself as antagonistic. The reference is established by capillary action. It puts order, its order, into the disparate, and the normative steamroller makes 'everything that resists its application appear as something twisted, tortuous or awkward' (Georges Canguilhem, *Le Normal et le pathologique*). The gap becomes a fault, and negligence or going off-track become subject to severe sanctions. This holds for both accounting norms and taxation law, something that recently disturbed a French legislator who knows America and likes it well, Pierre Lellouche:

> An obscure Franco-American fiscal agreement will transform our ministry of finance into an extension of the US Internal Revenue Service. This agreement translates into

French law an American law (the so-called FACTA) that obliges our financial institutions to declare to the US authorities all accounts held by American citizens or entities in France (100,000 Americans live here), when their balance is greater than €50,000. But without reciprocity: what the French tax authorities hand to the IRS, the American Treasury will not do in return, since US law does not permit it.

Our inspirers certainly accept that other societies do not want an exclusively American view of the world, as witness the preference of TV viewers for local series, provided that their little stories are told in the established form, which is taken for granted; provided that the documentary, even on so-called cultural channels, is fifty-two minutes long and not a minute more (eight minutes of commercial advertising); that the talk show, the anchor man and the advertising spot have due priority. They know that the French prefer a biopic on Piaf, de Gaulle or Dalida to one on Frank Sinatra, General Patton or Kennedy. What matters is respect for the genre, after which, everyone is free to follow their own taste. The same thing for the 'best of' or the 'pitch'. Format comes first, content follows. This is the primacy of manner over matter, everyone able to speak *globish* in their own language. At the Fête de l'Humanité in 2016, the anglophone masters of big beat led the family gathering, and none of those attending found anything amiss. Each epoch has its 'Internationale'. Ours is no longer signed Eugène Pottier, but Michael Jackson. In 1956, the US embassy was careful to explain that Coca-Cola was a firm ally in the struggle against Bolshevism, and there could be no question at La Courneuve of discussing the bright future (in the voice of Francesca Solleville)[6] with a glass of soda in the hand. In

---

6 The Fête de l'Humanité, organized by the French Communist Party and its newspaper, in its heyday a major cultural event, since

2016, the Atlanta company established a bottling plant in Gaza, at the express invitation of Hamas. What André Breton today, without inviting ridicule, would repeat the master's words from 1949?

> The United States, nothing is more foreign to me than their tacky pragmatism, nothing disgusts me intellectually like their invention of *Digests*, nothing revolts me so much as their superiority complex. I abominate their stranglehold over Central and South America. Forced to note that their imperialist design extends to the Old Continent, I fervently deny that the stupidity of Coca-Cola, its directors and its bankers, can prevail over Europe.

As Bob Dylan put it, *The Times They Are a-Changin'*.

The software simply follows from the material, and the material has no need of a Goethe or Confucius Institute to boast the exceptional merits of its inventors. The Estonian president for ten years, Toomas Hendrik Ilves, a former computer programmer, brought his country technologically into line with Skype, Twitter and Internet, everything American for both civilian and military purposes. As President Eisenhower already recognised, jazz was the best ambassador for America, at a time when a vinyl disc was easier to obtain than a Chevrolet (also a packet of celluloid), long before digitalisation brought emotive waves in the reach of every purse, and music became the most consumed content on the Net. The Red Army choirs, who sported their red flag across Europe, got ovations in the Palais des Sports, but did not enable cheek to cheek. What the 'slow' [= slow dance number] brought together was not peoples but bodies, penetrating in

---

1960 held in the Parc des Sports at La Courneuve in the northern suburbs of Paris. The singer Francesca Solleville (b. 1932) has always actively supported the political left.

the first person singular, which from the 1960s began to mean the many. Sarah Vaughan's 'Lullaby of Birdland' on 45 rpm was more than epic. Mystico-visceral. Billie Holiday, Elvis, Ray Charles ('Georgia'), Pink Floyd and many other magical voices, without their knowing, had an action at a distance that had begun with silent cinema, as Marcel Mauss had noted in 1934 in 'Techniques of the Body', evoking 'the social nature of habitus':

> A kind of revelation came to me in hospital. I was ill in New York. I wondered where previously I had seen girls walking as my nurses walked. I had the time to think about it. At last I realized that it was at the cinema. Returning to France, I noticed how common this gait was, especially in Paris; the girls were French and they too were walking in this way. In fact, American walking fashions had begun to arrive over here, thanks to the cinema.

Habitus varies with conventions, modes and prestige, and is the 'work of collective and individual practical reason, rather than, in the ordinary way, merely the soul and its repetitive faculties'.

We can attribute to this transfer-manic rationale the impregnation by ricochet (or the influence exerted by an initial fertilization on later products) of our ceremonies great and small. At the Invalides, these now conform to the model. Édith Piaf and Barbara have replaced the orchestra of the Garde Républicaine; children are in the front rows, and the names of the civilian victims of a dreadful accident are read out, to whom the Republic pays the homage formerly offered only to soldiers and resistance fighters who died in battle. Armies, too, have fallen in line, and pride themselves on being 'one of the best military segments of the NATO machinery in Europe', in which English is obligatory above the rank of colonel and the prevailing slogan is 'interoperability', respect for norms (Link

16 radio, for example, for data transmission on the Rafale fighter plane). Given the decline in our forces (by at least half in the army and three-quarters in the number of tanks), we have to show ourselves to our allies as transparent, reactive and interchangeable. We share therefore in the worship of miracle technologies, leaving the 'human factor' far behind. Strategists bothered by this are not well viewed by their hierarchy. 'The Atlantic drift of our model of forces', noted General Vincent Desportes, 'is deadly. One of the structural problems of the French armies is that they have progressively adopted the American strategic culture, but are incapable of giving themselves the tools for this. By dreaming American, the French army will wake up in its socks!' Another general hoped to see a reduction in 'the gap of a decade that always separates the development of concepts in the United States and their adoption by European armies'.

Our presidents adapt their use of time to canonical priorities, more useful to athletes and actresses than to submarine commanders and professors of classics. With their timetable constraints, they have to concentrate on what matters and counts: journalists, performers, economists and cameramen. Either you are serious or you are not. Teach only what is profitable, training for the skills of tomorrow. Bearing in mind, that to teach John mathematics you have to start by knowing John, and immediately afterwards, if possible, the rule of three (a rather offhand abstract of 'pedagogism', a method imported from the United States, where it is the guideline in primary and secondary levels, to many people's great regret). Newspeak turns to transcript: flexibility, adaptability, employability, opportunity for all, zero tolerance, and so on. Those particular characteristics of ours that we believed were firmly rooted, almost our heritage, stand out like a sore thumb. The same with secularism. The public authorities have removed it from the requirements of the blackboard and reason. It is learned like the regulator of sales offers on the health market, charged with protecting the self-service of beliefs, along with fair play, in the context of a free and fair competition between religious denominations. As for the Catholic Church, this adapts as best it can to the Protestant and Pentecostal wave: removal of pious images, banalization of the priest, moral generalities, reduction of liturgies and sacraments to the most simple. Charismatic renewals. Ecumenical gatherings. Everyone a priest!

Herod and the zealots

Examining how conflicts between civilizations proceed over the long run, the prescient Arnold Toynbee (who would probably have given Samuel Huntington a very low mark) identified two types of response by the weak to the strong – whether ancient Egypt faced with Hellenic colonization, the Jews faced with Roman occupation, or Islam confronted by the West (after the last war); the 'Zealot' and 'Herodian' responses. Herod the Great (*regnabat* 37–4 BCE), the client king of Judea, ruled under the control of the Roman governor. The Zealots, the last to resist Roman occupation, withdrew to the Masada fortress, where they killed one another rather than fall into the hands of the enemy (73 CE).

> The 'Herodian' is the man who acts on the principle that the most effective way to guard against the danger of the unknown is to master its secret; and, when he finds himself in the predicament of being confronted by a more highly skilled and better armed opponent, he responds by discarding his traditional art of war and learning to fight his enemy with the enemy's own tactics and own weapons. If 'Zealotism' is a form of archaism evoked by foreign pressure, 'Herodianism' is a form of cosmopolitanism evoked by the self-same external agency.

The Herodian is mimetic but not creative, from a concern for effectiveness. The Zealot, in the Maccabean tradition, is sacrificial but not calculating, from a concern for integrity. He is capable of charging with spears and shield against a machine gun, or, like the Poles in 1940, with his cavalry against a panzer division. The choice is finally 'between conformity and extermination', as Toynbee notes, not hiding a certain esteem for the man of reason who 'faces the present and explores the future', making 'a combined effort of intellect and will in order to overcome the "Zealot" impulse, which is the normal first spontaneous reaction of human nature to the challenge.' Nor does Toynbee conceal the tragedy of the dilemma. 'The rare "Zealot" who escapes extermination becomes the fossil of a civilization which is extinct as a living force; the rather less infrequent "Herodian" who escapes submergence becomes a mimic of the living civilization to which he assimilates himself.' The Masada option is to save one's honour but to die in the process. The Flavius Josephus option is to save the future, but by denying oneself. The memory of Masada is an example of moral heroism, and Flavius Josephus, the Jewish historian who changed sides and rallied to the Romans, an example of intellectual efficacy, since he was able, after passing to the enemy, to consign and transmit Jewish history to future generations, as well as attenuating the fate of his people by the influence he had with the emperor. The intellectual, the man of influence, who needs an audience on whom to exert his powers, is by vocation Herodian, since he has to tame the establishment and adapt to the surrounding milieu in order to be heard by this and carve himself a small place. The vocation of the Zealot or the Maccabee is rather that of the writer and the hermit, a St Genet or St Francis, men of solitude, who need to take their distance if they are to reach the end of their path. *Ad augusta per angusta.*

A draconian choice: Herod was indeed a puppet, but he ensured the Jewish people a certain prosperity, collected sufficient funds to rebuild the Temple and construct public baths and bridges; the extremist party of Zealots formed a short-lived Jewish republic, which drove out or put to death collaborators, but its leaders were soon exterminated, and the Temple rebuilt by Herod was burned down by Titus.

It is clear that the Brussels empire has chosen the Herodian path. Apart from the fact that the human organism has a remarkable plasticity, NATO-ized Europe does not lack circumstantial reasons for adapting to the world as it is, according to the principle: 'It is always right not to rebel.'

1) Challenging the established order demands moral and psychological resources provided only by a deeply anchored religious conviction. Faith moves mountains; scepticism leaves them in place. Would Armenia still be Armenian without Christianity, or Laos Laotian without Buddhism? A great cultural homogeneity is needed in order to balance a centrifugal force. We Europeans have already given what we can. The spring is broken, and a tree is not reparable. *A minima* negotiation of wines and cheeses better suits the state of our moral forces.

2) The die is cast, and it is useless to say no to the forward march of progress, of which the digital transformation of everything is the cutting edge. This is orchestrated from Silicon Valley, and is beyond our control (as much as the automobile, cinema and aviation were yesterday). Hegel himself taught us that it is foolish to want to stop the course of the sun, which, like freedom, goes from east to west, from Asia initially (only one man, the despot, is free), pauses for a while in Europe (some are free, aristocrats and bourgeois), and culminates in America (everyone is free). The sages of our tradition give us good advice on this matter. 'The fates lead the willing, they drag the unwilling' (Seneca), and we do not want to remain behind. Freedom, said Spinoza, is simply the recognition of

necessity. Since ceaseless rejuvenation of the world is the rule, obeying the inexorable call of the future, we simply make a wise use of our freedom.

3) The historical examples of 'Zealotism' are in no way attractive. Resistance to Romanisation was the act of small borderland kingdoms that were not especially well placed (besides Judea, compare the fate of Jugurtha, Hannibal, Massinissa, Zenobia, and so on). And the Zealots of the last century were finally no more than delayers – Québécois, Palestinians, Vietnamese – or, more commonly, pathetically shipwrecked – Communists and Third World-ists – and, in the worst case, terrorists and barbarians in the process of liquidation – al Qaeda, Islamic State and others. If your taste runs to reviving dictatorship, famine or kamikaze, better keep a low profile and tread softly. All the worse for the spectacle.

4) Of two repugnant options, we have to choose the least, and not make a wrong choice of ally. There is no question between France as *wilayah* or an 'associated free state' like Puerto Rico. We should not repeat the error of the Byzantine Christians, who in 1453 rallied to the besieging Ottomans as they found the Latin Christians intolerable and arrogant. 'Better the sultan's turban than the pope's tiara. With the former, we can at least preserve our identity.' The crushing status of American women may annoy us, but far less than the crushed status of Muslim women.

5) The Romanisation of Gaul was globally positive, particularly for the comforts of daily life that it brought those occupied and co-opted. Compare the wooden huts of the Allobroges with a two-storey Gallo-Roman villa such as was discovered on the Rance in 2016, with its heated rooms and baths, its colonnaded galleries, its walls and ceilings painted and covered with shells. This may well have been constructed to a standard

model, but I doubt that the owners complained that the architecture was in an imported style.

Tragedy arises, as we all know, when both sides have right on their side.

The dream then is for a third party to undertake negotiations with the ineluctable, inch by inch and without lowering arms. What this would need would probably be the intelligence of a Herod combined with the character of a Zealot. Something that does not grow on trees.

7

Why Is 'Decadence' Pleasant and Indispensable?

Because these moments are not only the most exquisite, they are also the most fertile. Having reached the best stage of fermentation, a civilization can then inseminate others, to which it will bequeath all or part of its original characteristics. Civilization is propagation. Decadence is transmission, hence rebound, hence survival. Mourning clothes not advised.

And what if Valéry's 'we other civilizations' put us on a false track? If his dictum that 'we know despite everything that a part of ourselves is immortal' was both more attractive and more exact? If dying, in this case, meant nothing more than a change? This thought might be impious with respect to our prophet-poet, who scorned any easy effects, but his unintended testament opened the way for a number of undertakers who are quick with their burial work. First of all, death is not an obvious phenomenon, and even for individuals its definition evolves or fluctuates. Until recently, it meant cardiac death, the stopping of blood flow; now it is brain death, the stopping of electrical circuits, which gives more time to 'repair the living' by organ donation (if the family consents in writing). A fortiori, the fatal moment will be harder to observe in a historical curve. As a general rule, the physiognomy, if it does not maintain a fresh complexion – except for cases of razing by fire and sword: Troy, Carthage, Alexandria – at least keeps up a presentable appearance, the custom of the spirit being to respect places. Knowing oneself to be mortal is commonplace; knowing oneself to be dying is more exceptional. Many death notices have proved to have a murderous intent, or at least to be over-hasty, each anticipating the stroke of midnight. Bernanos dated the end of Christianity from the day that compulsory military service was introduced, 'a totalitarian idea if ever there was one', he wrote, and saw the end of civilization in general with the advent of machinery and engineers who no longer believed in the superiority of his mother tongue (he had just learned that at the first meeting of the United Nations at San Francisco, French would no longer be the language of diplomacy). These mood shifts or fits of spite suggest circumspection.

The real question is to know what can and will survive of what surrounds and sustains us. Philopoemen was an exemplary general, who died at Messene in 182 BCE, and whom his Roman contemporaries liked to present as 'the last of the Greeks', worthy of a final salute to settle the account. But no more than Roman law, the bible of the West, gave up the ghost with the sack of Rome, did philosophy, a Hellenic invention, disappear with the battle of Pydna, when the Greek army was routed in 168 BCE. The syllogism, the theatre and the isosceles triangle, all born under the light of Attica, continued their paths both north and south. The meter of Greek poetry crossed into Gregorian plainchant, and later into the cantatas of Olivier Messiaen. Just as the three elements of the Roman triumphal arch, a thousand years later, reappeared in the porches of Romanesque and Gothic cathedrals. The relay has no foreseeable end. Rome died and was reborn in Byzantium, which was reborn in Moscow, the third Rome. Every empire will perish and leave new seeds, the American just as formerly the Roman (New York already seems rather provincial alongside Shanghai). But sooner or later it combines with another, in unexpected forms, rather than slipping into nothingness. California will be the link between the Atlantic axis and the Pacific basin, just as the Mediterranean once was between the civilized Orient and the Atlantic world. Manhattan will be reconstructed still more photogenic than before (Berlin and Warsaw offer good examples). The Statue of Liberty, sadly amputated, will have its torch restored, Trump Tower likewise, and Chinese tourists will be the first to demand the reopening of the Taj Mahal casino in Atlantic City, now classified as a historic monument. Only cultures can become extinct, like a language in an Amazonian clearing or a Himalayan valley when it ceases to be spoken. From the death throes of Latin came the weak creoles of Italian, French, Portuguese, Spanish and Romanian, yet each of these became the vehicle of great literature. It is specific to civilization to bear within it a gene capable of hybridization. It does not die without children, whether legitimate or merely natural. Nothing dies; all is transformed. This nothing that is everything is the hard kernel, which we can call its spirit, in Paul Valéry's words, or its soul, after François Cheng. The Chinese spirit, the Indian spirit, the European spirit and others again will not disappear into a great void. Since when did the death of an individual, or a collective one, put an end to the laws of heredity or the long-term becoming of the species, the kingpin? 'Nothing of what is', said Péguy, 'ceases one fine morning to be what it was' – nor, we might add, to inhabit what will be, so that the past is unfinishable. Nineveh and Babylon disappeared with the Assyrian empires, but not the Mesopotamian chronologies found in the Bible; the logogram, then cuneiform, gave rise to the consonant alphabet of Aramean, and after the fall of Ugarit, to the vocalic alphabet of the Phoenicians, followed after the decline of Byblos by the Greek alphabet. And I myself heard Aramaic, the language of Jesus, spoken at Maaloula near Damascus. Pearls give rise to strange pearls, but there is a thread and it is the thread that matters. Just as there were always ancestors before our ancestors, so we are and will remain heirs, with potentially other heirs, even if we do not know whom.

Are we not, on our promontory, an example of this inexplicable and tireless conservation instinct still worthy of attention? Post-Christians that we are, even anti-Christians, we have remained Christians without knowing, just as the anti-Roman Christians of the past still remained Romans. Rising against Rome, they founded the 'apostolic, Catholic and Roman' church. And we French secularists are likewise Catho-secularists, concerned for unity, homogeneity and a well-defined corpus that requires a legal framework. As for yesterday's revolutionaries who set off to storm Heaven, did they not have a Great Promise as their springboard? Our modern philosophies of history are converted theologies, which call salvation revolution. The repertoire of holy war, of martyrs whose blood will be seed, of heresies to be punished, traitors to be unmasked, a party that strengthens itself by purging – all this did not spring from nothing. Who said that our legacy was not preceded by any testament? We descend from the New Testament in a straight line. We have reconfigured the eschatological expectations of millenarianism, and the bitter experiences of the progressive twentieth century had their preamble in the defeated Crusaders. There was a bloodbath, but the regeneration did not happen; the evil is still with us. The 'great day' left us in the lurch. The idea of a radical break between the new man and the old, between the old covenant and the new, with an élite of the elect to guide the flock to a future it would be unable to find by itself – that is Lenin, but originally it was St Paul. It is hard, we can admit, to abandon the idea that history has a direction and not simply a course, and that tomorrow could well be made of a different stuff than yesterday. Without the dogma of the Incarnation, without the idea of a history inhabited by the Spirit, a Christ who is the word and promise at the heart of the world, would we still have a stake in the games of princes struggling for world domination? Would we still take so much interest in the ups and downs of the kingdoms of the world? Christian civilization underlay our own quest, giving it a background of unease that a Buddhist or an Epicurean, each separating the spiritual from the temporal, would most likely find incomprehensible, and very damaging for the serenity of the spirit.

What then leads our reluctance to accept the baggage of the human caravan, among which is the slowing coming to a close of an expiring existence, a state known as decrepitude?

Because we really love catastrophes.

Erosion, which is the objective law of nature, has in our eyes the fault of not inspiring dreams. Being good neither for thinking nor imagining, it is doubly vexing for our misplaced vanity, and we flee the commonplace for grandiose curtain-falls. A good ending, worthy of a disaster film or a comic book, requires the anger of God or Sardanapalus, the Fellinian orgy, tongues of fire, the exterminating angel. Rather the precipice than the steady slope. Heroes do not wear themselves out; they fall shattered. Mere unravelling humiliates, apocalypses exalt. In the absence of Attila, the image of Tartars coming to water their horses at the fountains of the Place de la Concorde was long very popular with Léon Bloy – 'I await the Cossacks and the Holy Spirit' – and our Surrealists. And the sunken Atlantis, the mysteriously deserted Easter Islands, Crete – the isle of King Minos, devastated by an earthquake after a thousand happy years – are still successful themes. The great religious stories well understand this proud need for horror (opera librettists also); Flood, Apocalypse and Last Judgement are key parts of our stock of mythologies. There is a pathos about the ultimate – 'better an end with horror than a horror without end' – which, among other merits, has that of aggrandizing the bearer of bad news. And anyone who proclaims in one breath the end of democracies, of the West, of America, of culture, of butterflies and beans, is sure of a good return from the media. Coming elections are treated as the last chance and final leap before the famous 'end of history', a misinterpretation of the origin of the phrase (by which Hegel meant the moment when human history discovers the truth of its ideal end, rather than the moment at which it stops). Which of us does not shiver at the mention of the Day of Resurrection, the opening of the Seventh Seal, the battle of Armageddon, or alternatively, of the final struggle, the 'last of the last', the event that will supplant all events?

This is not the way that things happen. A gradual slippage, a slow retreat or crumbling away, are far more real as phenomena, once we look closely, than are civilizations killed off suddenly by sword-thrust, gunpowder or cholera. Sudden bankruptcy and general collapse may well be admissible hypotheses, but they are far less likely. Declivity is synonymous with mediocrity. Collapse is great; decline is petty. It is 'declinist'. Unacceptable. In fact, it is a declining and already well Americanized Europe, held to the obligation to be 'positive' and 'remain young' (the metropolis does not like the diminished and the fatigued), that sees 'declinism' in public life as akin to paedophilia in private: an offence against good manners, combined with a sin against hope. It is seen as unhealthy, if not criminal, to want to know what happened at Athens after the arrival of the Romans, at Madrid after the golden age, at Vienna after 1918 or in Europe today. The sign of a dark and dejected soul. The subject of study is supposed to have a bad influence – on the student first of all, then on the curious as well.

This is magical thinking. Does the examination of funerary rituals encourage the death drive, gerontology a disgust for life, or universal gravitation the desire to jump out of the window? The obligation to face the future with the frank and resolute gaze of the Boy Scout requires that rise is never followed by fall, that eyes be veiled against the troughs between the peaks that are always evident. We take care, for example, not to see the present-day proliferation of museums as a sign that we have indeed entered into the aesthetic age, more suited to connoisseurs and collectors than to fire-stealers; the age of ironies and little peeves, of grandstanding, when each person secretly believes themselves above everything they say and do. The clinical balance-sheet of subsidence, however, is an open secret: the multiplication of public holidays, the invasion of circus games, the rise in incredulity, territorial dismemberment, dissociation between moral authority and political power, the crumbling of the state, the rise of each for themselves, and so on. There is no need here to beat our breasts. Nor to blacken a moment of transition between what germinated with us and will flower again elsewhere and differently. How can new civilizations emerge if older ones do not leave them a bit of room? Unless the grain dies . . .

Why does this smell of sulphur attach to what is misnamed decadence, but often sees effervescent broths of culture, and even the gilded peak of a trajectory that has had time for cross-fertilization with sufficient heteroclite contributions to make an accomplished hybrid? To again quote Paul Valéry:

> The age of civilizations must be measured by the number of contradictions they accumulate, by the number of incompatible customs and beliefs that meet up and temper one another, by the plurality of philosophies and aesthetics that coexist and often mingle in the same head.

We might add that twilight is conducive to talent. And that well-hung meat releases subtle aromas just before decomposing. Rome was never so innovative as in the age of the Antonines. The splendour of the city was at its peak, as was that of its ports and provinces; philosophy, theatre, the novel (Apulius) and poetry were all at their best, just when anarchy was beginning to decompose the Pax Romana. The Spanish golden age was the apogee of imperial construction before its collapse; eighteenth-century France, in the last years of the

Ancien Régime, was a firework display; and it took two centuries for the Portuguese impress to fail, from the Lisbon earthquake of 1755 to the Carnation Revolution of 1974. The three blows of the final act generally take their time. But the finest example of these autumnal flowerings, these creative ferments of old age, was that of Vienna between 1870 and 1930, the decrepit head of the Austro-Hungarian empire, the final successor of the Roman Empire in the West, after five centuries of existence. Everything went from bad to worse in this country after its defeat by Prussia at Königgrätz, torn apart by nationalisms from within, with a court hobbled by dramas and suicides, and an emperor who became a mere puppet, the very time that Vienna was becoming the capital of the objective spirit of the Western world. Behind the masks of operetta and waltzes, Mayerling and Sissi, Vienna's high culture laid the foundations for all the century's new inventions. And this great epoch began curiously enough in 1871, exactly when the political and military centre of continental Europe passed from Vienna to Berlin, forcing the imperial crown to abdicate any dominant role on the international stage. *Finis Austriae*, in the European arena, prefigured *finis Europae* on the world stage, and this dress rehearsal could inspire us, having not only illuminated its own century, but gone on to fertilize the next. We are all still children, if not parasites, of the Ring, the Vienna Circle, the cafés, galleries, clubs, reviews and cabarets – the agencies of this irreplaceable 'decadence'. The Viennese *Who's Who* of the Belle Époque includes half the pantheon of the year 2000. In painting, Klimt, Kokoschka, Schiele. In architecture, Adolf Loos, Otto Wagner. In music, Alban Berg, Gustav Mahler, Arnold Schoenberg, Anton Webern. In human sciences, Sigmund Freud, Ludwig Wittgenstein, Joseph Schumpeter, Wilhelm Reich. In literature, Robert Musil, Stefan Zweig, Hermann Broch, Karl Kraus, Manès Sperber. In cinema, Fritz Lang, Josef von Sternberg, Erich von Stroheim, Michael Curtiz. Hollywood would not be what it is if it had not received these civilizers, no more than would London, Harvard and Paris. What 'ism' cannot be preceded by the prefix 'Austro'? Zionism, Marxism, positivism, expressionism, and so on. Who has said that leaving the stage of history is a cause for depression? On the contrary, in these celebratory and conclusive periods, a melancholy of the heart does not prevent gaiety of spirit; times in which the art of living is taken so far that some people can live from art and for it; when it is no longer necessary to hope in order to take action, even by way of thanks; when, convictions having lost their blinding force, the real is revealed to people's minds with neither addition nor disguise; where corsets are loosened and caps fly above prohibitions. The collective loses, the individual gains. Decadence, some will say; liberation, say others. And why not both?

When life has taught us that it is impossible to cheat one's inheritance in the long run, it is doubtful whether a saffron robe and Buddhist sandals can do other than what we have not chosen but cannot cease to do. All we do, at the end of the day, is *continue*. This is vexing in one sense and comforting in another, as it follows that a continuation in the future is not impossible.

This is known as transmission. It is a long adventure, in which smiling ultimately prevails over a moment's tears.